A Self-Esteem Self-Help CBT Workbook for Adults

Breaking Free From Social Anxiety, Self-Doubt, and Stop Toxic Thoughts to Increase Confidence With Proven Exercises and Practicing Radical Self-Love

Franceene Christenson

© **Copyright 2022 - All rights reserved.**

The content contained within this book may not be reproduced, duplicated or transmitted without direct written permission from the author or the publisher, **PublishingFish Inc.**

Under no circumstances will any blame or legal responsibility be held against the publisher, or author, for any damages, reparation, or monetary loss due to the information contained within this book, either directly or indirectly.

Legal Notice:

This book is copyright protected. It is only for personal use. You cannot amend, distribute, sell, use, quote or paraphrase any part, or the content within this book, without the consent of the author or publisher.

Disclaimer Notice:

Please note the information contained within this document is for educational and entertainment purposes only. All effort has been executed to present accurate, up to date, reliable, complete information. No warranties of any kind are declared or implied. Readers acknowledge that the author is not engaged in the rendering of legal, financial, medical or professional advice. The content within this book has been derived from various sources. Please consult a licensed professional before attempting any techniques outlined in this book.

By reading this document, the reader agrees that under no circumstances is the author responsible for any losses, direct or indirect, that are incurred as a result of the use of the information contained within this document, including, but not limited to, errors, omissions, or inaccuracies.

Get your free gifts here

https://publishingfishinc.aweb.page/p/bdb7793b-db9d-4e8a-b7b6-e512f5be99be

Table of Contents

INTRODUCTION: CBT CAN SET YOU FREE 1
    EXERCISES 3

CHAPTER 1: CHANGE IS POSSIBLE—CBT CAN HELP 5
    WHAT IS CBT? 6
    HOW DOES CBT WORK? 7
    WHO CAN CBT HELP? 8
    HOW TO BEGIN USING CBT 8
    TAKEAWAYS 10

CHAPTER 2: KNOWLEDGE IS POWER—LEARNING THE COGNITIVE TRIANGLE 11
    WHAT IS THE COGNITIVE TRIANGLE? 12
    ROLE-PLAYING 13
    HOW CAN THIS HELP YOU? 14
    TAKEAWAYS 17

CHAPTER 3: BREAK THE CHAIN—UNDERSTANDING THOUGHT CHAINS AND AUTOMATIC THOUGHTS 19
    WHAT ARE AUTOMATIC THOUGHTS? 19
    HOW DOES IDENTIFYING THEM HELP? 21
    TAKEAWAYS 25

CHAPTER 4: BETTER THOUGHTS, BETTER LIFE—OVERCOMING THINKING DISTORTIONS 27
    WHAT ARE THINKING DISTORTIONS? 28
        Common Thinking Distortions 28
    HOW DOES KNOWING ABOUT THEM HELP? 31
    TAKEAWAYS 34

CHAPTER 5: CHALLENGE TO CHANGE—CREATING NEW CORE BELIEFS 37
    WHAT ARE CORE BELIEFS? 37
    EXAMINING YOUR CORE BELIEFS 39
    CHANGING CORE BELIEFS 40
    TAKEAWAYS 43

CHAPTER 6: PUSHING THE LIMITS—EXPOSURE THERAPY 45
    WHAT IS EXPOSURE THERAPY? 46
    STEPPING OUTSIDE YOUR COMFORT ZONE 46
    TAKEAWAYS 50

CHAPTER 7: UNDERSTANDING WHAT MATTERS—DISCOVERING YOUR VALUES AND FACING CRITICISM 53
    WHAT ARE CORE VALUES? 54
    HOW IDENTIFYING VALUES SUPPORTS SELF-LOVE 55

  STAYING TRUE TO YOUR VALUES 59
  TAKEAWAYS 63

CHAPTER 8: POSITIVITY FOR CHANGE—FOCUSING ON THE POSITIVE 65

  NEGATIVE MENTAL BIAS 66
  LOOKING AT THE POSITIVE 68
  TAKEAWAYS 72

CHAPTER 9: RISE TO THE CHALLENGE—PROBLEM SOLVING WITH CBT 75

  THE IMPORTANCE OF PROBLEM-SOLVING 76
  THE CBT METHOD OF PROBLEM-SOLVING 76
  TAKEAWAYS 81

CHAPTER 10: NEW HORIZONS—SETTING GOALS THE CBT WAY 83

  THE IMPORTANCE OF GOALS 83
  SETTING SMART GOALS 84

TAKEAWAYS 89

CONCLUSION: GOING FURTHER 91

  BOOK TAKEAWAYS 93

REFERENCES 95

  IMAGE REFERENCES 96

Introduction:

CBT Can Set You Free

They always say time changes things, but you actually have to change them yourself. —Andy Warhol

I used to read books just like this one. I studied psychology in college, but I didn't read self-help psychology for class. I was reading it because I wanted to help myself. I was suffering from severe social anxiety and very low self-esteem. I was seeking out help to live a better life from every resource I could find.

It was a long journey to get to where I was in college, when I finally started to seek help. I am sure you have been struggling for a while, too. Problems like low self-esteem and social anxiety are not created in a flash. They won't get better quickly, either.

But, they do get better. The quote at the beginning of this introduction gives you a hint at how to change your life. You have to make a change. Tools like this workbook can help, but change begins with *you*.

Let me tell you my story and show you that change is possible. This is *my* story, but I am sure you will recognize it. Everyone who struggles with low self-esteem and social anxiety can relate to similar feelings. And, everyone who struggles with these things can benefit from the same help.

I played alone as a child and never had many friends, but that wasn't too bad. Lots of kids start out as loners. My mother used the phrase "late bloomer" to describe me. This led me to think that my problems would go away in time. I thought that one day, I would wake up and be a blooming flower, brimming with confidence and ready to make lots of friends.

That was not the case. My struggles only got worse when I started high school. I went to a much larger school than I had before, and I started to become very uncomfortable around others. Many people go through struggles with self-love and feeling socially awkward as teenagers, but my problems went beyond that. They got worse. I didn't even want to go to classes or see anyone socially because of my anxiety. And it kept getting worse.

I had my first panic attack in a crowded, loud auditorium during a school assembly. I was terrified to be around that many people and to still feel so alone. I felt like I didn't fit in with anyone. I ended up running out of the room as fast as I could. This only made me feel more embarrassed when I realized the whole school saw me do it. From that moment on, I was deeply critical of everything I did. I lived in fear of people watching and judging me.

I, like many people, continued to hope that my problems would solve themselves over time. Maybe I just hadn't bloomed yet. I dreamed that college would be a time when I opened up. I imagined I would move away to a small school and really become myself. I knew that, on the inside, I had potential; I just had no idea how to go from the person I was to the person I felt I could be.

Going to a campus where no one knew me, and reinventing myself, was my biggest dream. But, when freshman year of college rolled around, I found myself facing the same issues. Time hadn't changed anything. I began to read self-help books and look for a way to make a change in my life, so that I could love myself and feel comfortable around others.

Cognitive behavioral therapy (CBT) was the single, most helpful tool for me. I first learned about it in an "introduction to psychology" class. When I discovered its emphasis on being your own therapist and helping yourself, I thought it might be a good way to try to overcome the social anxiety and lack of self-confidence that was holding me back in so many ways. I bought several books on CBT, including a workbook with exercises.

These books became my constant companions. I read each one at least twice. As I worked through each workbook, I was noticing small, but measurable improvements the entire time. I slowly started to reframe my thoughts about others, the world around me, and even myself. This reframing opened up new possibilities for me and reduced my anxiety.

I tried CBT, and it worked. Of course, it didn't work overnight. I had to put in the effort and spend a lot of time doing workbook exercises and reading up on the subject. I kept journals and monitored my thoughts, and I planned and problem-solved (all things you'll be doing in this workbook). Little by little, my social anxiety eased, and my confidence grew. I saw a dramatic change in myself between my freshman and sophomore years. I was so impressed with the power of CBT and the psychological principles I had used, that I decided to make psychology my major.

This workbook was born, not only from my BA in psychology, but also out of a lifetime of observing and researching human behavior. I have always tried to learn as much as I can about how the mind works. I know that the tools in this workbook are effective because I have successfully used them; and, I have seen them work for others, as well. I believe so strongly in CBT that I am writing this book to try to help as many people as possible. I truly believe CBT can help you, just as it has helped me and millions of other people across the world.

This workbook details the exercises and techniques that were most useful to me and that I have seen help others suffering from social anxiety and low self-esteem. I have presented them to build on each other. The techniques and concepts from one chapter lead you into the new ones in the next. You can skip around if you like; the techniques will be useful no matter what order you read them. However, if you do jump around, some chapters may contain concepts that are unfamiliar to you if you haven't read the previous chapters.

I know you are struggling, even suffering. I know, because you wouldn't be reading this book if you didn't feel like you needed help to live your best life. I can tell you that it does get better. I have felt it get better. I have seen it get better. You can learn to love yourself and be free of social anxiety. CBT can help you to do just that.

My lack of self-love and struggles with social anxiety began when I was young, and I was lucky to learn about these CBT tools when I was still in college. But, whatever stage of life you are in, you can find help. This book will share examples of people from all stages of life who have used these techniques to overcome their struggles. There is no "can't teach an old dog new tricks" when it comes to CBT. In my research, I have even seen seniors learn to love themselves and reduce their social anxiety after a lifetime of feeling anxious around others and battling low self-esteem.

Anyone can learn and apply the skills and concepts in this workbook. CBT was founded on the principle that people can retrain their thinking and help themselves live better lives. Even when guided by a therapist, CBT is centered around the client coming up with their own answers and solutions, based on the techniques their therapist teaches them. This workbook teaches some of those same techniques.

If you ever feel that your struggles are too much, or that you need more specific and individual help than you can get from this workbook, reach out to a mental health professional. CBT can be aided by a therapist, and a professional's perspective can add valuable insight. You can even bring this workbook to your therapist, if you choose to go that route.

If you're ready to dive in and get started on your journey toward radical self-love and freedom from social anxiety, then keep reading. The first chapter teaches you a little about the basics of what CBT is, and how you can apply it to reduce your anxiety and learn to love yourself. We'll also discuss how to use this workbook and get the most out of the exercises.

Exercises

This is a workbook, so each chapter will include exercises that will allow you the opportunity to practice the CBT skills that you are learning. Take the time to do them as you read. They are a large part of this workbook, and they will help you take CBT from conceptual learning to practical application. Normally, the exercises will appear within the text, set aside by bullet points.

The following are a few exercises for this introduction. Take the time to answer these questions and consider your answers. Hopefully, reading my story will help you think a bit about your own journey up until this point. These questions will also be good to refer back to, if you need a motivation boost while working with CBT.

1. What aspects of social anxiety and low self-esteem do you struggle with the most?

_____
_____
_____

2. What led you to pick up this workbook and try CBT?

_____
_____
_____

3. What do you hope to gain from CBT?

_____
_____
_____

Chapter 1:

Change Is Possible—CBT Can Help

At any given moment we have two options: to step forward into growth or to step back into safety. —Abraham Maslow

Maslow is one of the most well-known psychologists of the twentieth century. His observations and his emphasis on treating people as *whole people*, rather than a collection of symptoms, were foundational to modern psychology and CBT. This quote shows his very astute mind at work.

We can move forward, toward change and growth, but even when where we are is bad, we may want to stay. It can feel safe, comfortable, and predictable to stay where we are and not change. Things may be hard, but we fear they will become even harder. So even when we struggle with issues like lack of self-love or intense social anxiety, change can be scary.

Congratulations on taking your first step forward into growth! Seeking change and taking action, like picking up this workbook, are big steps on your journey toward self-love and freedom from social anxiety. This journey can be a bit overwhelming, and even scary, but I assure you it is worth it.

CBT has worked for millions of others, and it worked for me, too. It can, and will, work for you if you keep taking steps toward growth. This workbook will be your guide as you begin your CBT journey. This chapter will help you understand what exactly CBT is, how it helps and, most importantly, how you can begin to put it to work for you.

What Is CBT?

I would define CBT as being the most evidence-supported form of therapy. It can help you grow confidence and self-love, while conquering toxic thoughts and social anxiety. All that is true, but it may not be the most helpful starting point. Let's look a little closer at CBT.

CBT stands for cognitive behavioral therapy. That means it is a therapy that focuses on our cognition (thinking) and behavior. Some forms of therapy center around thoughts and may focus more on working with a therapist to sort out those thoughts, personal history, and even unconscious thoughts—in the form of dreams and desires. Other types of therapy focus heavily on the therapeutic aspect of a particular behavior. This includes art therapy or even animal therapies, where a relaxing and meaningful behavior is used to help the therapist teach a client to cope with challenging emotions and situations.

CBT focuses on changing thoughts and behaviors, equally. Both are seen as important, and different CBT techniques center on either thoughts or behavior. The main idea behind CBT is that we can change our thinking and our behavior with conscious acts of will and the application of the right technique.

CBT doesn't mention feelings as much. That might seem strange, because negative feelings are often the primary reason people seek therapy in the first place. It was the main reason I started reading self-help books. I'm sure, if you're reading this workbook, you have unpleasant feelings you want to get rid of; however, there is a very simple reason CBT focuses on thinking and behavior, rather than feelings.

Have you ever tried to *make* yourself feel differently? I know I have. I used to tell myself things like, "I won't be scared to go to this crowded lecture class." However, when I showed up to the class, nothing was different. I still felt very anxious and uncomfortable, with sweaty palms and a racing heart. There is a reason for this. Feelings are outside the control of our willpower.

If people could just will their negative feelings away, then we wouldn't need workbooks such as this one, and CBT would never have been invented. That is not to say your feelings can never change; they most certainly can. But, it is important to change your feelings by changing your behaviors and your thoughts.

This is because we do not have a conscious choice over our feelings. However, actions and thoughts are within our voluntary control. The emphasis is on working with the things you can control, to influence the things you cannot directly take control over. Because of this, CBT focuses on thinking and acting differently, so we can *do* things that help us to feel differently.

- Consider CBT's stance on thoughts, behaviors, and feelings. What do you think of it? Are you willing to try to change your thoughts and behaviors to change how you feel? Spend a few minutes thinking and writing about your initial thoughts on CBT.

_____
_____
_____
_____

How Does CBT Work?

You may notice that the other types of therapies mention a therapist and a client. Don't worry. You won't need to find a therapist to use this workbook or practice CBT. That is another unique aspect of CBT that has made it one of the most widely used forms of therapy in the world.

If CBT is worked on with a therapist, they will act as a guide who helps the client take steps to change their thoughts and behavior. The person seeking help comes up with all their own solutions and does all the work for themselves. This self-help approach isn't accidental. It's part of how CBT was designed, and a large part of why it is so effective for so many people.

By encouraging you to help yourself, CBT makes you self-reliant. This self-reliance is the main reason that CBT has such dramatic, long-term gains. Because the skills CBT teaches are within your own power and are techniques that you learn to practice, you can help yourself, in most situations. By learning CBT skills, you can take them with you wherever you might go, and use them no matter what may arise.

CBT was founded on four basic principles. First, problems are caused partly by unhelpful thinking patterns. Second, problems are also caused by unhelpful behaviors that result from unhelpful thinking. Third, both of these unhelpful ways of thinking and behaving have been learned. Finally, it is possible to learn new, helpful ways of thinking and behaving. When these new ways are used in place of the old ways of thinking and acting, problems will be reduced and eventually eliminated.

CBT works in several ways. The first is by teaching how unhelpful thoughts and behaviors arise, what they look like, and how to recognize when they are happening. The second is to teach us how to stop, change, or replace those unhelpful patterns of thinking and behaving to create positive change in our lives. Finally, the third helps by showing us useful and logical ways to tackle life's stresses, such as problem-solving and goal-setting. The key to CBT is that people are encouraged to learn these things for themselves, and to act as their own therapists.

Who Can CBT Help?

CBT has been proven, through years of research and clinical evidence, to help with a variety of problems. In addition to the issues of self-esteem, social anxiety, and toxic thinking that this workbook focuses on, CBT can also help with depression, generalized anxiety, PTSD, and some substance abuse issues. The reason CBT can be applied so broadly is that it does not address specific problem thoughts or behaviors but, instead, focuses on what helpful thinking and behavior look like. By providing positive models and tools, CBT can help people overcome a wide range of different problems.

The main reason CBT can be so effective for such a wide variety of struggles is the emphasis on learning and finding your own solutions. CBT does not teach a one-size-fits-all solution to our problems. Instead, it is a combination of principles about thinking and behavior that help to implement a set of techniques we can use to arrive at unique solutions to our personal problems.

The exercises in this book are aimed at helping people who want to increase their self-love and self-esteem, while decreasing social anxiety and toxic thinking. There is a wealth of CBT techniques and exercises available. One workbook couldn't begin to fit them all. Some exercises are aimed more at different types of problems, but all of them focus on unlearning old, detrimental behaviors and thought patterns, while learning to implement new, helpful thoughts and behaviors.

How to Begin Using CBT

As you begin your journey with CBT, it is important to start by noticing your thoughts and behaviors. The key is to recognize which ones are leading to problems and which ones might be helpful to you. Even if you think you aren't engaging in any helpful thoughts or behaviors, that isn't true. You are reading this workbook, which is definitely a helpful behavior. And, if you are looking for help, then you are having the beneficial thoughts that change *is* possible and that you *can* reduce your suffering.

There are a few things you can do to increase your awareness of your thoughts and behaviors. To help me notice my negative thoughts and actions when I first began using CBT, I kept a journal where I wrote down the toxic things I *thought* and *did* that I believed caused me problems. I didn't do this to dwell on them. I did this to better remember them and analyze them later.

I also made notes on the things I did which I thought were helpful. This served to encourage me and keep me going when I felt like giving up. At first, there weren't a lot of things I recognized I was doing right; but, as I began using CBT techniques, I was able to note down the times I utilized my new skills and write about how they helped.

Journaling while using this workbook can be an excellent way to see how much progress you are making. It is also a good way to repeat workbook exercises. During my CBT journey, I kept two journals. The first was the record of my thoughts and actions that I mentioned earlier. I did this in a small notepad I carried with me, but your phone's note-taking app is another great option. The second journal I kept was a larger one where I would journal each night about my day, and repeat any workbook exercises I wanted to do again.

If you are unfamiliar with journaling, don't worry. The process doesn't have to be daunting. Simply set aside a few quiet moments at the end of each day to record how your day went, what you thought about, and any difficulties or successes. Keeping track of your days allows you to look back and reflect on how CBT is helping you and where you are applying it in your life. You can use a journal both to track improvements you've made and identify areas you want to continue to work on.

- If you plan on using a journal with the workbook, make a plan now. Write out *when*, for *how long*, and even *where* you will journal. This will help you form a habit, and make it easier to find the time to do it.

_____
_____
_____

Your journal can also be used to repeat exercises from this workbook. CBT is like anything else; practice helps you improve. Fill out the exercises in the workbook first, and if you want to repeat them, you can use your journal to do them over, as many times as you find helpful. Repetition can really help make it easier to change your thinking and cement new ideas into your mind.

Doing the work is a huge part of CBT, but learning the principles of how we think, act, and (as a result) feel is the other key part. This workbook will introduce a useful CBT principle, or two, in each chapter. I'll teach you about different ways of thinking—both good and bad—and about types of behaviors. After you've learned about a new CBT principle, you'll get exercises that will put what you learned into practice and get you started using the new information from each chapter to improve your life.

- Make a commitment to help yourself with CBT by doing the work. Write out a contract with yourself that you will do your best to help yourself by applying the skills in this workbook.

    I _____(name) will do my best to use CBT and this workbook to help myself overcome social anxiety and increase my self-love. I will practice the exercises and apply CBT techniques to better my life and improve my self-esteem.

    Signed _____ (signature)

    On _____ (date)

A *takeaways* section will appear at the end of each chapter to summarize key points. That way, you can quickly flip to the back of any chapter to refresh yourself on what you learned, and review the new CBT techniques presented. These sections won't replace reading the chapter in full, but they will help you refresh yourself, and jog your memory if you want to go back and review a chapter without having to reread the whole thing.

Takeaways

- CBT stands for cognitive behavioral therapy. This means it focuses on thoughts and behaviors.

- People can learn to help themselves using CBT, and CBT was designed for people to do just that.

- CBT is proven to help with a wide range of struggles—including social anxiety, low self-esteem, depression, and negative thinking.

- To begin using CBT, become aware of your thoughts and behaviors. A thought record, simply a place where you write down your thoughts and actions, is a great way to form the awareness CBT requires.

- It will be helpful to keep a journal as you work with this book, to track your progress and see how your life changes. You can also use this journal to repeat workbook exercises.

In the next chapter, we'll dive into a foundational principle of CBT called the cognitive triangle. It describes how our thoughts, behaviors, and feelings are interrelated. You'll also get started doing some exercises that will help you begin to replace toxic thoughts and behaviors with more positive, helpful ones.

Chapter 2:

Knowledge Is Power—Learning the Cognitive Triangle

You are today where your thoughts have brought you; you will be tomorrow where your thoughts take you. —James Allen

If you pause and think, I'm sure you'll realize that this statement holds a lot of truth. You are here, right now, reading this workbook because your thoughts have brought you to a place where you are seeking help. At the same time, your thoughts and actions have brought you to a place where you are ready to help yourself.

You can change your life in major ways just by changing your thoughts. Your thoughts influence both your feelings and behavior. Feelings and behavior also influence thoughts. This is demonstrated in a CBT concept called the "cognitive triangle," which is especially helpful for dealing with the negative results of social anxiety and toxic thinking.

For this chapter's exercises, think of a time that you wish things had gone differently. Pick a situation where you have some control of your own reactions. Start small, while you practice the cognitive triangle, and then move on to more impactful situations.

For example, I used to avoid going out with acquaintances when invited, and made excuses to stay home. Write out your situation here.

- My situation:

_____
_____

What Is the Cognitive Triangle?

Imagine a triangle. Don't worry. You won't have to find the hypotenuse or solve for x. Just think about how each of the three points is linked to each other. In the cognitive triangle, each point is represented by an aspect of our lives that impacts our mental well-being. The three points of the cognitive triangle are thoughts, feelings, and behaviors.

Just as the points of a triangle are linked, so are our thoughts, feelings, and behaviors. This is easy to understand, if you think about it for a moment. When you think toxic thoughts, you end up feeling bad; and, when you think positive thoughts, your feelings also reflect that.

Behaviors come into play, too. When you do something that is good for you—for example, get some exercise—you often feel better, and you typically think more positive things. If you do something that is bad for you, like procrastinating on housework, you often feel bad about yourself or the situation, and you end up thinking more negative thoughts. The same is true for feelings. When you feel bad, you are more prone to think toxic thoughts or to engage in negative behaviors. The opposite is true when you feel good.

We often find ourselves in feedback loops. These loops result when one of the aspects of the cognitive triangle influences the others and those, in turn, continue to influence all the way around the triangle. Because of this effect, it can be difficult to change our feelings, thoughts, and behaviors without making a conscious effort. CBT teaches us how to go about making those efforts so they will be the most effective.

The cognitive triangle is the foundation of CBT. If you change your thinking or the way that you act, then your feelings are going to change as a result. As we talked about in the first chapter, feelings can't be changed by willpower or choice. This means that, in CBT, we focus on the two points of the cognitive triangle that are within our control: namely, our thoughts and our actions.

In later chapters, we will discuss specific ways to change our thoughts and behaviors. For now, simply realize and reflect on the influence that each point of the cognitive triangle has on the others. Try to observe it in your own life and look for links between thoughts, actions, and emotions. It may even be helpful to journal out a few situations in which you see how these three components influenced each other for good or bad in your life.

- Write down your initial thoughts, feelings, and behaviors about the situation you wrote down earlier.

Thoughts:
_____
_____

Behaviors:
_____
_____

Feelings:
_____
_____

- Example:
    - Thoughts: *No one will like me if they get to know me.*
    - Behaviors: *I refuse to join in social activities.*
    - Feelings: *I feel lonely and sad.*

Role-playing

Role-playing is a CBT technique that we will use throughout this workbook. All you need to do to engage in CBT role-playing is use your imagination. Role-playing means thinking and imagining a scenario to find different possible outcomes and strategies for approaching a situation. You can role-play by yourself by simply using the cognitive triangle to think about what thoughts or behaviors you could change in a situation, that would change how you feel about it. The exercises at the end of this chapter will get you started.

Other chapters will also have role-playing exercises in them. You might even be asked to solve a problem or apply a technique to a situation that isn't your own. This can be a helpful form of role-playing, because you can practice CBT techniques without your feelings being involved. That way, you can see how the techniques can work without worrying about a situation where a lot of emotion might cloud your thinking. Role-playing out scenarios that aren't your own is also a great way to practice CBT and get more used to thinking in the new ways this workbook will teach you.

If you have a trusted friend, you can also role-play together. This is not uncommon, at all. Many people practice things like job interview questions with knowledgeable friends. If you know someone else who might benefit from CBT, you could even work through this book together and use role-playing to get new perspectives and ideas about your struggles. If you do a role-play with a friend, make sure it is someone you trust enough to share the situation you are role-playing with and who is not involved in it. That way, they can offer honest ideas and feedback without their own emotions coming into play.

Therapists are other people you can engage in role-playing with. If you have a therapist, you may even have already tried role-playing with them. If not, you can always ask them to try it with you. They can act as the other person in a situation, which allows you to practice what you want to say or express and see how that person might react in real time. This type of real-time role-playing can also be done with a friend who is not involved personally in the situation.

How Can This Help You?

Knowing that our thoughts, feelings, and behaviors are all linked and influence each other means we can pick one or both of the two that are within our control and use it to impact our entire lives. If you choose to change your thinking about a situation, then it will make it easier to behave in a different way. That change in thinking and behavior will change how you feel about the situation. If you choose to behave differently, then your thoughts and feelings will begin to change, as well. And, if you do nothing differently, then—as I know from experience—your life will remain mostly the same.

I know a man we'll call *Ryan*. He unexpectedly lost his job a couple of years ago. Initially, he spent a lot of time looking for a new one. But, early in his job search, he got two very painful rejections back-to-back. This resulted in him taking a major hit to his self-esteem. After these rejections, he began thinking things like: *I am not good enough to get any job* and *I'll just get rejected; what's the point in trying?*

Ryan spent a month not looking for a job. During that time, he mostly engaged in avoidance behaviors: watching television mindlessly, sleeping too much, and overeating. Ryan eventually saw that he was not going to find a job without looking, and he started to worry about his financial situation.

Ryan began to seek help from self-help books. When Ryan learned about CBT, he realized that his feelings weren't likely to change unless something else did. He applied the cognitive triangle, and took control of his thoughts and behaviors in the hopes of improving his self-esteem.

Ryan began looking for a job again, even though he didn't feel like it. That was his change in behavior. In combination with this, he changed his thinking by focusing on finding a new job, not as a burden or a series of rejections, but as a chance to try something new and take on a challenge. These two changes were within Ryan's control. He made renewed efforts to find a new job, and he actively caught himself when he started thinking in unhelpful ways.

Change didn't happen overnight, but new behavior and thoughts shaped how Ryan felt about himself and his job search. Soon enough, his self-esteem began to improve, and it was evident in the fact that his interviews were going better and causing him less extreme anxiety. When his self-esteem improved and Ryan looked at finding a new job as a challenge, not a chore, he put in even more effort. Eventually, he landed a new job that he finds much more satisfying than his last one.

- Now write out the links you see between these three aspects of your situation.

My thoughts cause me to feel:

_____
_____

My thoughts cause me to act:

_____
_____

My behaviors cause me to think:

_____
_____

My behaviors cause me to feel:

_____
_____

My feelings cause me to think:

_____
_____

My feelings cause me to act:

_____
_____

- Example:
    o My thoughts cause me to feel: *Anxious to open up to others.*
    o My thoughts cause me to act: *In a way that keeps me isolated.*

- o My behaviors cause me to think: *That I must be very awkward.*
- o My behaviors cause me to feel: *Isolated and lonely.*
- o My feelings cause me to think: *I will never have friends.*
- o My feelings cause me to act: *Socially distant from others.*

- What would happen if you changed your behavior?

_____
_____
_____

Example: *If I changed my behavior, I would accept an invitation to spend time with new people. That would cause me to feel anxious, but I might also have some fun. I would feel less isolated because I would not be spending all my time alone. I might find out I like these new friends.*

- What would happen if you changed your thinking?

_____
_____
_____

Example: *If I began to think that I was not awkward and considered that people might like me if they got to know me, I would feel less anxious in social situations. This would make it easier for me to accept invitations and spend time with my new friends.*

- Use the cognitive triangle to role-play a recurring situation. See if you can think about a new thought or behavior to try when the situation comes up again.

Situation:
_____
_____

Past thought:
_____
_____

Past behavior:
_____
_____

New thought:

_____
_____

New behavior:

_____
_____
_____

Once you try your new thought and behavior, write about how it changed your feelings about the situation.

New feelings:

_____
_____

Use these cognitive triangle exercises to change your thoughts and behaviors in a way that positively impacts your feelings. The cognitive triangle is a key technique you can come back to again and again to change patterns of behaviors and thoughts in your life. Repeat this exercise in your journal whenever you need to change the way you feel about something.

Takeaways

- Thoughts, feelings, and behaviors all influence each other. CBT calls this group of interactions the cognitive triangle.

- In CBT we learn we can change our thoughts and behaviors to help ourselves feel better. We focus on thoughts and behaviors because we can control them through our will. Emotions are outside the realm of willpower to control completely and healthily.

- The cognitive triangle exercise shows how you can choose to act and or think differently about a situation to break negative cycles and feel better.

In the next chapter, we'll look at thought chains, a CBT tool to help you change your toxic thoughts. With awareness, time, and a bit of effort, you can even change the thoughts that happen automatically so you can continue to feel and act differently.

Chapter 3:

Break the Chain—Understanding Thought Chains and Automatic Thoughts

One cat just leads to another. —Ernest Hemingway

Automatic thoughts are a lot like cats. They can be hard to control, and it feels like they do as they please. This chapter is all about identifying your automatic negative thoughts, and learning what other thoughts and behaviors they lead to. This will help you take control of your thinking to consciously influence how you act and feel.

What Are Automatic Thoughts?

Automatic thoughts are exactly what they sound like. They are the thoughts that happen in an instant, without having to come up with or focus on them. Here we will deal with automatic negative thoughts because those are the ones that cause us trouble. The automatic positive and neutral thoughts we have are generally not an issue.

Thought chains are the resulting series of thoughts that come from an automatic negative thought (sometimes called an ANT.) Some people describe a negative thought chain as "spiraling out." This phrase accurately describes the sinking and repetitive feelings that go along with a repeated negative thought chain.

- Identify your thought chains. Start with an event that led you to feel bad about yourself. Choose an everyday event, not something very big. For example, I used to feel terrible about myself when I got a bad grade in school. Write down your automatic thought and the thoughts that followed it, until you get to the thought that caused you to feel bad or engage in unhelpful behavior. Think about the thoughts between the automatic negative thought and your bad feeling. What were they? Did they assume the automatic thought was true and accurate?

Inciting event:

_____

_____

Automatic thought:

_____

_____

Thought 1:

_____

_____

Thought 2:

_____

_____

Thought 3:

_____

_____

Thought 4:

_____

_____

Thought 5:

_____

_____

Feeling:

_____
_____

These thought chains often end in unhelpful behavior that is the result of unchecked negative thinking. These unhelpful behaviors can be a wide range of things. In the case of social anxiety and low self-esteem, they are often avoidance or negative self-talk.

Our thoughts also have a huge impact on how we feel. So, even if we avoid taking harmful actions, we still feel bad when we get caught in a negative thought chain that results from automatic negative thinking.

It is possible to take control of these thought chains. CBT can help you learn to interrupt, reduce, and even eliminate them. The key to doing this is to identify when an automatic negative thought happens.

Once you've identified that an automatic thought has occurred, you must evaluate that thought instead of immediately believing it to be true. Recognizing, understanding, and challenging our automatic negative thoughts can help prevent damaging thought chains.

Stopping our automatic negative thoughts and the chains that result from them allows us to feel less anxiety and more self-love, because we are looking at the good and the bad in a situation instead of focusing our thoughts on the negative. We'll even talk more about how we focus on the negative, and how we can use positive thinking to steer us back toward realism, in a later chapter.

How Does Identifying Them Help?

CBT encourages us to be aware of and try to change our automatic negative thoughts. When we have an automatic thought, we don't evaluate it. Instead, our first impulse is to assume that it is realistic and true, but this isn't always the case. Many times, our automatic negative thoughts are clouded by thinking distortions.

We'll cover thinking distortions in the next chapter. For now, what's important is simply to ask if an automatic thought is realistic or if it is clouded by negativity. Automatic thoughts that are colored by a negative view of the world are the ones we will work with and correct throughout this chapter.

- Look at your thought chain. Ask yourself if each thought is rational, or if it is unrealistic. I realized in college that my thoughts about my bad grades weren't rational. One "C" did not mean that I was stupid, and even a "D" didn't prove that I would never earn my psychology degree. Circle the thoughts above that aren't realistic. Now, think of a new, more balanced thought to replace it with. I changed, "I'll never be smart enough to earn a degree" into "I need to try harder on my other tests and maybe ask for help if I am stuck." Write down your more balanced thoughts here.

Realistic thought 1:

_____
_____

Realistic thought 2:

_____
_____

Realistic thought 3:

_____
_____

Realistic thought 4:

_____
_____

Realistic thought 5:

_____
_____

Realistic thought 6:

_____
_____

- Consider how the new thoughts make you feel. Does seeing things more realistically help you build your confidence? Does a new thought lead to a new feeling for you?

    New feelings:

    _____
    _____

- Remember that, in CBT, we change our thoughts and behaviors to change our feelings. What new or different behaviors might reinforce your new, realistic thoughts? List some ideas here and try to engage in at least one of them. I chose to set aside a certain time each day to study for a couple of hours, even if I didn't have a test. This new behavior helped me build confidence and reinforced my new thoughts that if I work harder, I can improve my grades.

- New behaviors:

_____

_____

When we are frequently thinking and believing negative, toxic thoughts without evaluating them, we damage our outlook on the world and our self-esteem without even realizing it. It is hard to feel good about life or to love yourself when your automatic thoughts are filled with unchecked negativity.

These automatic negative thoughts are often the result of well-worn paths of thinking. We develop automatic thoughts when we think the same thing over and over, about similar or related situations. Often, the result is that we have the same thoughts when presented with a similar situation, whether or not those thoughts really fit the facts. It is possible to change automatic negative thoughts through awareness and repeated correction.

CBT can help. I have a friend, James, who has very poor self-esteem. One day over coffee, he confided in me that any time he gets a compliment, he immediately assumes that the person "doesn't mean it" or that they are "just being nice." I identified this as an automatic negative thought and told James a bit about CBT. I suggested he watch out for his automatic thoughts for a while, and the results were surprising.

When we met up again, a few weeks later, James told me he was realizing that he often had automatic negative thoughts that he believed to be true. These sent him into thought chains that damaged his self-esteem on a daily basis. James didn't always engage in hurtful behaviors as a result of these thought chains, but the continued negative thinking was still taking its toll on how he felt about himself.

But, even becoming aware of how much of his thinking was automatic, was helping. James chose to continue working on CBT and evaluating his automatic negative thoughts. He kept a thought record and regularly engaged in thought stopping.

Thought stopping is a technique where you force yourself to stop a certain pattern of thinking. You choose a silent, personal cue that you will use to remind yourself to redirect your thoughts when you start in a negative thought chain. James chose to think of a large red stop sign. Whenever he started to spiral into a negative thought chain, he would catch himself, think of a stop sign, and then consciously force himself to think about an entirely different topic.

You can practice thought stopping in the same manner. Just choose a thought to be your cue. Then, whenever you find yourself in a negative thought pattern that is leading you to a negative space, think of that cue. Make it something simple and distinct. After you have thought about your cue for a few seconds, change your thoughts and focus on a new topic. It is most helpful if this topic is something positive or enjoyable, and unrelated to the thought chain.

- If you plan to work with thought stopping, think of a *cue thought* to use when you need to stop a thought chain. It should be something specific and simple. It also helps if it resonates with you personally or symbolically. Some people choose stop signs, red traffic lights, or a simple phrase like, "Stop it, Franceene," to cue them.

My cue:

_____
_____

James kept a list of possible topics on his phone. When he had to thought stop, and he had the time, he would look at the list. He'd pick a topic of interest that he enjoyed and, sometimes, took a few minutes to read about it on the internet, while staying away from negative news or comments. This practice helped James get better at distracting himself, and ensured that the negative thoughts weren't able to quickly return, because his mind was occupied with something else.

- Come up with some topics you can redirect your thoughts to when you thought stop. James would often think or read about baseball. I usually think about my favorite authors and books, or consider what I might crochet next. List a few things you can distract your mind with.

  Topic 1:

  _____
  _____

  Topic 2:

  _____
  _____

  Topic 3:

  _____
  _____

As a result of this work with CBT, James started to grow in confidence and self-love. His other friends and I saw the change in his demeanor and personality, as he flourished into a more confident person. James credits a lot of his personal change simply to the awareness of his automatic negative thoughts and the work he did to stop them.

Practicing the exercises in this chapter will help you grow in confidence and self-love. They are the same ones I showed to James. You can use them over and over, if you like, to identify and work with your automatic negative thoughts. Repetition will make it easier to catch these thoughts before they lead to thought chains and damaging behavior.

Like the cognitive triangle exercise, the thought chain analysis exercise is worth doing multiple times, for different automatic thoughts or situations. Learn to recognize your automatic thoughts and ask if they are realistic. If they aren't, try to consciously replace them with more balanced ones. Practice thought stopping when negative thought chains threaten your mind. Don't forget to redirect your thinking when you thought stop, or you may find yourself slipping easily back into the same negative thought chain you tried to interrupt.

Takeaways

- Often our automatic negative thoughts are distorted and unrealistic.

- However, we usually assume they are true because they come to us so easily.

- This means that automatic negative thoughts can lead us down a path of negative thinking that results in unhelpful behavior and unwanted emotions.

- When automatic negative thoughts occur, we damage our self-esteem, increase our anxiety, and make it harder to feel good and take positive actions.

- Use thought-stopping to interrupt your automatic negative thoughts and, once you have stopped, focus your mind on something else to keep you occupied. This refocusing will help you not fall back into the same thought chain you tried to stop.

- Consciously create new, more balanced thoughts and use them to counter your automatic negative thoughts. This will help you feel better and see things more rationally.

In chapter four, we will look at some specific ways our thinking, especially our automatic thoughts, can become distorted and unrealistic. These common themes of unrealistic thinking are what CBT calls thought distortions. We'll also talk about how to counter those distortions with logic and reasoning so that we can think, feel, and act in more helpful ways.

Chapter 4:

Better Thoughts, Better Life—Overcoming Thinking Distortions

Change your thoughts and you change your world. —Norman Vincent Peale

Our thoughts shape our perception of the world and make our experience of it. We all experience reality as filtered through the lens of our own personal experience and outlook. Because of this, it stands to reason that distorted thoughts would lead to a distorted view of both us and our world. That's natural.

It is also natural to have distorted thoughts. They are so common that CBT has labeled and named over 30 types of distorted thinking. Part of the reason for this is that our minds have a bias toward the negative. We'll discuss combatting this negative mental bias in a later chapter.

For now, we'll work with thinking distortions and how unrealistic thinking can impede self-love and lead to increased anxiety. First, we'll define thinking distortions, then look at several that commonly affect self-esteem and social anxiety. Finally, we'll work on ways to clear up thinking distortions, and practice taking distorted thoughts and formulating realistic, logical thoughts to replace them.

The exercises in this chapter will give you practice in identifying thinking distortions, so that you can catch them and correct your thoughts before too much damage is done. As with all CBT skills, practice makes perfect; so, repeat these exercises in your journal, if you like.

What Are Thinking Distortions?

Thinking distortions are what CBT calls the common ways in which our thinking becomes unrealistic and illogical. These thinking distortions are similar to the logical fallacies you may have learned about in argumentation, but they happen in our own minds.

In CBT, we are able to name and label thinking distortions into different categories, because people fall prey to the same types of logical errors in thinking. This is a good thing, and it means we can easily develop tools to challenge each type of thinking distortion, instead of looking for new methods of challenging each distorted thought that causes us problems.

In this section, we will look at a list of common thinking distortions. This list is not exhaustive. CBT currently identifies over 30 types of thinking distortions. CBT is focused on self-help, so complete lists of cognitive distortions are available for free online. You can look them up, if you are interested.

I have chosen only a few for this list. I wanted to keep things from getting too long, and to make sure to have enough time to clearly explain and provide examples for each type of distortion listed. Since this workbook focuses on the realms of social anxiety and self-esteem, I have chosen the thinking distortions my research has shown to have the most impact on those issues.

Common Thinking Distortions

- Personalizing: Personalizing is when you believe an event, that may or may not be directly related to you, is personal. For example, if your date gets a phone call and has to leave, assuming it is because they didn't like you and wanted to end the date, that is personalizing. If they don't have a history of this behavior, it is just as likely that they had something unexpected come up.

- Mind reading: Mind reading is when you guess or decide that you know what someone else is thinking, based on any evidence other than them telling you what they are thinking. Mind reading occurs when you think you know what someone is thinking based on their tone of voice, the look on their face, or any other indirect cue. These signs point to emotions, not specific thoughts.

- Negative predictions or fortune-telling: We make pessimistic predictions when we overestimate the odds that something will turn out negatively. As a result, we generate anxiety about the imagined outcome, and may even engage in avoidance behaviors. If you assume a job interview will go poorly, because you have had bad interviews in the past, that is fortune-telling. Your past job interviews do not have an impact on how the next one will go, so you cannot use them to logically predict the outcome.

- Catastrophizing: Placing a greater emphasis on, or assigning a greater weight to, a negative event than it warrants is called catastrophizing. If my friend doesn't text me back in a few hours, it would be catastrophizing to think that this was a sign that they no longer wanted to be friends. Catastrophizing leads to increased anxiety and emphasizes negative, and less likely, scenarios over more likely and benign scenarios.

- Overgeneralization: It's easy to overgeneralize. We do this by drawing broad conclusions from specific events. For example, my thoughts of *I did badly on this test; I must be stupid* were overgeneralizing. A grade on one test does not reflect the entirety of anyone's intelligence. A good way to check for overgeneralization is if you are thinking with words like "never" or "always." It is a good sign that you are drawing very broad conclusions when you use language like this. It is not logical that anything holds true all, or none, of the time over a wide variety of situations.

- Jumping to conclusions: Jumping to conclusions occurs when we interpret one situation to have more significance in relation to some other situation than it logically does. The thoughts I shared, about believing that my bad grades in freshman year meant I would never finish my degree, are a prime example of jumping to conclusions. I took a specific situation like a single test grade and extrapolated an entire academic career from it.

- All-or-nothing thinking: This type of thinking is exactly as it sounds. When you think that things must be all one or all the other, with no in-between or nuance, you're engaged in all-or-nothing thinking. Keywords that point to all-or-nothing thinking include *always, never, every time,* or *every* (event, type of person, etc.). This type of distorted thinking often leads to unrealistic expectations and dissatisfaction when things are not entirely the way we want them to be. Just because it rained for part of the morning, doesn't mean that there was no sun in the afternoon.

- "Should" statements: Should statements are any thought that involves how you, someone else, or the world "should" be. These kinds of statements lead to expectations that are hard to meet, and cause frustration and disappointment. In this regard, they are similar to all-or-nothing thinking. The idea that "everyone should be nice" is great as a personal value—but as an expectation, it is unrealistic. You know that not everyone you meet will be nice, regardless of what you think they should act like. Another danger of should statements is applying them to yourself. If you think *I should always be friendly*, that creates an unfair expectation that you cannot always meet. No one is always friendly, and you might get disappointed or hard on yourself when you naturally fail to meet that expectation.

- Learn the thinking distortions in practice by coming up with an example of each from your own life and then writing a more realistic, undistorted thought that you can use instead.

Personalizing:

_____
_____

New thought:
_____
_____

Mind reading:
_____
_____

New thought:
_____
_____

Fortune-telling:
_____
_____

New thought:
_____
_____

Catastrophizing:
_____
_____

New thought:
_____
_____

Overgeneralization:
_____
_____

New thought:

_____
_____

Jumping to conclusions:

_____
_____

New thought:

_____
_____

All-or-nothing thinking:

_____
_____

New thought:

_____
_____

Should statement:

_____
_____

New thought:

_____
_____

How Does Knowing About Them Help?

Understanding the types of thinking distortions can make it easier to catch yourself when your thinking becomes distorted. If you have practiced and learned the common types of distortions, you can quickly see them in your own mind. Labeling something helps you to identify it easily when you see it again later. This is very true for thinking distortions.

Once you are able to identify them, you will also be able to learn what types of corrections can be made for each distortion. All thinking distortions are a sign you need to stop and re-evaluate, but different ones can be handled with different antidotes. For example, overgeneralization can best be countered by considering outliers and exceptions to the generalization you have just made. Should statements, on the other hand, can be countered by rewriting them with some nuance to create a more balanced and fair expectation.

Regardless of the exact thinking distortion, the best counter is always balanced and realistic reasoning. Most thinking distortions result from thinking with too much emotion and ignoring our reasoning. It is not a good idea to repress or ignore emotions, but they should not run the show. I always remind people that emotions are our navigators and reasoning should be our pilot. That way, we listen to our emotions when they are helpful, but let our reasoning make the final decisions about our thinking and behavior.

- Keep a record of your negative thoughts for a few days. List them in your journal or on your phone. Take the time to identify what thinking distortions are at work. When you are done with your record, identify your most common thinking distortion and think about how you can best combat it.

My most common distortion:

_____
_____

I can argue with it by:

_____
_____

As you learn and work with CBT, you will discover various specific methods to counter thinking distortions, and learn which ones work best for you. The simplest breakdown of how to counter any thinking distortion is a four-step process. First, identify and label the thinking distortion. If you don't know a specific name for it, then describe how your thinking is being distorted and what is illogical about the thought.

The second step is simple. You stop. Take a deep breath, or do something else that helps you form a mental break point. Third, begin to correct the distortion. Take your original thought and bring it more in line with objective evidence, so it can be more realistic and accurate. Finally, use your new thought and consciously argue against, and replace, the original distorted thought if it begins to crop up again.

- For more help in understanding thinking distortions, look at some of these common, negatively distorted thoughts. Try to identify what distortion is at work in each one, and offer a more realistic thought for the situation.

"She didn't call me back. She must hate me."

Distortion:_____

New thought:

_____
_____

"The interviewer didn't shake my hand. They think I'm terrible for the job."

Distortion:_____

New thought:

_____
_____

"I know this presentation is going to go badly."

Distortion:_____

New thought:

_____
_____

"I failed my test. I'll never pass this class."

Distortion:_____

New thought:

_____
_____

"I should always look happy in front of others."

Distortion:_____

New thought:

_____
_____

"Men always treat me badly. I shouldn't bother dating."

Distortion:_____

New thought:

_____
_____

"If I can't get this job, then I should just give up in this industry."

Distortion:_____

New thought:

_____
_____

"My boss didn't say hi when I saw them at the cafe. I'm sure it's because they don't like me."

Distortion:_____

New thought:

_____
_____

Sometimes you will have negative thoughts, and that is okay. Thinking distortions aren't about always being entirely rational, or eliminating your emotional mind. Instead, they are a way to help you learn to skew your thoughts back toward the rational and realistic when they become so negative that they are creating problems in your life.

Takeaways

- Thinking distortions are common ways in which our thinking becomes irrational and skewed toward the negative.

- There are over 30 identified thinking distortions in CBT.

- Some thinking distortions that commonly lead to social anxiety and low self-esteem include: personalizing, mind reading, fortune-telling, catastrophizing, overgeneralization, jumping to conclusions, all-or-nothing thinking, and should statements.

- Knowing about these distortions helps you to quickly identify and correct them.

- Once you identify a distorted thought, you can consciously create a more realistic, undistorted thought that will help you feel better and act from a balanced perspective.

In the following chapter, we will talk about core beliefs. Just like our daily thoughts, our basic beliefs about ourselves, others, and the world we live in can be distorted to reflect an unrealistic view of life. Using what you now know about thinking distortions and emphasizing rational thoughts, we will analyze your core beliefs and start setting them into balance so you can live a happier and more satisfying life.

Chapter 5:

Challenge to Change—Creating New Core Beliefs

The moment you doubt whether you can fly, you cease forever to be able to do it. —J. M. Barrie

Our beliefs shape what is possible for us. We often fail to see options because we view the world in a particular way, and those options may seem impossible even when they are, in fact, available to us. CBT calls the beliefs that we hold to be most true about the world, others, and ourselves our core beliefs.

These beliefs often determine what we consider possible, and what we feel we are capable of achieving. We may not be able to literally fly as the characters in *Peter Pan* do, but if we have a core belief that we are unable to do something, we rule out any chance of ever doing it because we will never even try.

In this chapter, you'll do exercises aimed at identifying and examining core beliefs. Once you've identified any distorted or unrealistic core beliefs, you will work on ways to replace them with better ones. Keep in mind that this work can take a while. If you want to do additional journaling to look at your core beliefs, repeat the exercises or do some writing on your own.

What Are Core Beliefs?

Core beliefs are the things we fundamentally believe are true. We usually don't question, or even think much about, our core beliefs unless something dramatic happens that causes us to question them. We can, however, make a conscious effort to analyze them. Core beliefs can be about ourselves, the world in general, or other people. They are deeply embedded in our worldview. In fact, you could even say they *are* our worldview.

Core beliefs are often formed very early in life. They remain somewhat flexible, and major events in adulthood can continue to shape them, but we start to create them as children. Because we form them so early, it is sometimes hard to know why we have a certain core belief. Teasing this out can sometimes be helpful—but in CBT, it isn't necessary. We will look at ways you can uncover the origins of your core beliefs later in this chapter, if you are interested in doing that work.

For the purposes of CBT and this workbook, all you need to do is identify what your core beliefs are. If you want to go deeper and uncover why, you can do some journaling and work out why you might believe certain things. However, to start changing core beliefs, you only need to identify them.

- To identify core beliefs, fill in the following statements without giving them too much thought. Use these statements to evaluate what you automatically think about the world, others, and yourself.

I am:

_____
_____
_____

Other people are:

_____
_____
_____

The world is:

_____
_____
_____

- I have found that automatic thoughts can point to our core beliefs. Look at some of the automatic thoughts you recorded previously in this workbook, or in your journal or thought record. An automatic thought can point to a core belief if it is repeated or very strongly believed to be true. Choose two automatic thoughts and write down what core beliefs support them. Then, consider if those beliefs are distorted and come up with new ones, if necessary.

Automatic thought:

_____
_____

Core belief:

_____
_____

Automatic thought:

_____
_____

Core belief:

_____
_____

The point of identifying core beliefs is to see if they are distorted. Core beliefs can become distorted, just like our automatic thoughts can. If core beliefs are distorted, they lead to distorted thinking and unrealistic expectations about the world.

These unrealistic expectations, whether they are good or bad, lead to dissatisfaction and unhappiness. That is because having an unrealistic expectation that is too high leads to disappointment. Having an expectation that is unrealistically low leads us to doubt or question the good things that we would otherwise enjoy.

Examining Your Core Beliefs

Examining core beliefs may sound like hard work. That's because it is. But, if you are reading this, then I can assure you that you're ready. You've been changing your thoughts and behaviors, and learning to free yourself from distortions in your daily thinking. Changing core beliefs is like a more advanced version of changing daily distorted thoughts. Think of it as a fun challenge, and a chance to uncover some things about yourself you may never have thought about consciously before.

The first step to changing core beliefs is identifying them. The exercises at the beginning of this chapter have already given you some ideas on how to do that. You can also start thinking, and perhaps journaling, about what you believe to be true about yourself, other people in general, and the world at large. Don't worry if you start this process and begin to realize that some, or even all, of your beliefs seem like they may be distorted. That's the next step.

You already know some common thinking distortions. Not all of them apply to core beliefs, but many of them can. For example, it is common for a distorted core belief to be a should statement, or for a core belief to overgeneralize yourself or others. Take a look at your core beliefs that you feel might be distorted. Can you identify a distortion? Even if you can't find a specific thinking distortion at work, your core belief may still be flawed.

- Look at the core beliefs you wrote down. Are they really true? Can you identify any distortions? Look for the use of words like "always," "never," or "should" to help identify distorted core beliefs. Circle any distorted beliefs. Now write new, more realistic core beliefs you can start to replace your old, distorted core beliefs with.

I am:
_____
_____
_____

Other people are:
_____
_____
_____

The world is:
_____
_____
_____

If your gut is telling you something is not right about a core belief, then examine it further. Try to weigh it in light of how realistic, balanced, and logical it is. If you find it is distorted or doesn't live up to your standards of being logical and helpful, then try to change it.

Changing core beliefs begins just like changing thoughts. Write out a new, more realistic, and helpful core belief. Unlike when changing thoughts, the results will take more time to see. You will likely have to remind yourself of this new belief very often, at first. In the next section, we'll go into more detail about how to work on replacing distorted core beliefs with new ones.

Changing Core Beliefs

The struggle with changing core beliefs is that, unlike automatic thoughts, they are not only recurring and automatic, but are also strongly held to be true. It will certainly take more time and effort to change a core belief than to change some thoughts, but the results are worth it. Know that the process takes time, and be kind to yourself while you work on reshaping your beliefs.

The benefits of changing core beliefs are even more dramatic than the benefits of changing your thoughts. Consider Sarah, who suffered from extreme social anxiety. Her therapist suggested that she look at what core beliefs might be at work, that caused her to be anxious around other people. She did exercises similar to the ones in this chapter and discovered the core belief that people are not trustworthy.

Sarah worked to change this core belief by reminding herself of people in her life she did trust, and times when her trust had been rewarded. She made a list of people she could trust and added to it every time she thought of someone else. At first, the list included mainly family members and a long-term friend; but, after thinking hard for a few days, Sarah was able to add a couple of newer friends and a coworker to the list.

She realized that more people had rewarded her trust than she initially thought. This work helped to change Sarah's core belief that people could not be trusted. In time, she realized her core belief was faulty, and she replaced it with a healthier belief that some people were worthy of her trust. This dramatically lessened Sarah's social anxiety.

Sarah later decided she wanted to know why she felt this way about people. She did some digging in her journal and with her therapist. Eventually, she realized her social anxiety began after the breakup of a bad relationship where a lot of lies were revealed to her.

This happened in her early twenties. Afterward, she became very distrustful. Sarah didn't need to know this to change her core belief, but further understanding of its origin helped her realize that she hadn't always held this belief. Realizing that this belief had not always been a part of her thinking helped Sarah to cement the new, undistorted core belief even more.

Notice that, in this example, Sarah worked with a therapist. The therapist was able to provide helpful insight and an additional perspective on Sarah's social anxiety. However, Sarah did the work following her therapist's advice and used exercises, similar to the ones in this workbook, to change her core beliefs. This is typical of CBT and goes to show that in CBT, it really is all about the client doing the work for themselves, to change their own lives and improve their own mental well-being.

Therapists can still be great guides and provide a lot of help, but they are not strictly necessary to work with CBT to improve your life. If you feel you need more personalized help than might be available with this workbook, you can consider seeking out a therapist yourself.

For me, the process of changing my core beliefs was similar. I believed people wouldn't like me if they got to know me. I knew this was the result of having been teased as a child by several people I had thought were my friends, but turned out to be very fickle.

I believed the same thing would happen with a variety of potential friends, throughout my high school and early college years. When I began to learn about CBT, I realized this was a core belief that I held, and more importantly, I realized it was damaging my social relationships and my self-esteem. I did a similar exercise to Sarah, and listed people who I knew liked me and things I thought were likable about me.

To begin challenging my core belief that I was unlikeable, I posted the second list on my bathroom mirror. I read it to myself every morning, and reminded myself regularly that I was a good and likable person. It took time, but slowly, as I looked for more evidence to challenge my old core belief, I began to find it. As I started to change what I believed about myself, my self-love grew and my social anxiety diminished.

- If you have unhelpful and distorted core beliefs, you should find a way to challenge them. It is often helpful to list evidence to the contrary, to challenge and change old core beliefs. Make a plan for what you will do to start challenging your distorted core beliefs and put new ones into action.

I will change my core beliefs by
_____
_____
_____

Changing distorted core beliefs has several benefits. Doing the work allows you to have fewer distorted thoughts on a daily basis. This is because our everyday thoughts arise from our core beliefs. When we make sure our core beliefs are realistic and free of distortion, our thinking is more likely to follow that pattern.

Another benefit to changing distorted core beliefs is managing your expectations. If you have core beliefs that lead to an expectation that things will go badly, or that life will be unpleasant, then you are starting from a place of anxiety before you even look at the actual situation. This kind of distortion forms a negative cycle, where you expect things to go poorly and then use confirmation bias to see evidence of life being unpleasant everywhere.

- Know your reasons. Changing core beliefs can be easier if you know why you want to change them. Knowing your reasons can give you the motivation necessary to continue working on changing core beliefs.

   I want to change my distorted core beliefs because:
   _____
   _____
   _____

If you want to, and feel up to digging deep, you can do some journaling about what the origin of your core beliefs might be. Only do this work if you feel ready and are curious. It is not essential to change core beliefs, but it can help you identify if there was a time that you did not have this belief, or if its origins may be rooted in a specific event from which you are overgeneralizing.

One helpful tool for finding the origin or reason behind a core belief can be the many layers of the "why" method. This journaling technique involves writing out a distorted or unhelpful core belief such as, "I believe that I am unlikeable," and then asking yourself why you believe this. Take some time to answer *why* in your journal, on the page you have labeled with the core belief you are investigating. Once you answer your first *why*, ask why you believe that answer. Keep going for five to seven steps of asking why you believe your answer to the previous question.

This technique helps you dig deeper into your thoughts and beliefs, instead of accepting the first answer you find. While your first answer is probably true, there is likely a more enlightening reason behind it. Because core beliefs are often old, and always deeply held, this kind of questioning process is a good way to get to the heart of them.

If you begin digging into the origins of your core beliefs and the work becomes difficult or triggering, seek out a therapist to work with or step back from it for a time. CBT doesn't require us to always mine the past to know why. It only requires us to make changes in the here and now.

Takeaways

- Core beliefs are how we see ourselves, others, and the world on a fundamental level.

- Just like thoughts, our beliefs can be distorted.

- Finding new, undistorted core beliefs takes time and work. You didn't develop your beliefs overnight, and they won't change overnight, either.

- Determining the origin of your core beliefs is not key to changing them. If you do want to find out their source, try the many layers of the *why* journaling technique, or freely question them in your journal.

- If you put in the time and effort to replace distorted core beliefs, it will be easier to view yourself (and life) in a more realistic way.

- Knowing your motivation to change your unhelpful core beliefs can make the work easier.

- This more realistic worldview helps lead to less anxiety and greater genuine self-love.

We've talked a lot about thoughts and beliefs up to this point. Next, it's time to put new thoughts and beliefs into action! In chapter six, you'll start working on exposure therapy. Don't be worried. It sounds a lot more daunting than it actually is. And, if you've come this far, you're definitely ready to engage in new behaviors.

Chapter 6:

Pushing the Limits—Exposure Therapy

If you opt for the safe life, you will never know what it is like to win. —Richard Branson

Entrepreneur Richard Branson was encouraging others in the business world with this quote. Still, it can be applied to life, as well as business. If we avoid the things that challenge us and cause us anxiety, we can't overcome those challenges, or feel the confidence and pride that results from facing our anxiety and growing beyond it. Exposure therapy is all about stepping outside of what you consider "safe" to experience those wins and gains.

The exercises for this chapter lead you through planning, implementing, and reflecting on your first trial of exposure therapy. But, remember that it takes time and repetition to really benefit from this kind of work. Use your journal to continue carrying out and reflecting on the plan you begin here. Keep going step-by-step, until you are comfortable engaging in your goal behavior.

What Is Exposure Therapy?

Exposure therapy sounds scary and it can be anxiety-inducing, but it is not dangerous. It just means exposing yourself to situations you know are safe, but that cause you anxiety, or that you have been avoiding for a similar unhealthy reason. Maybe you avoid crowded situations, or perhaps you are too anxious to talk to new people at get-togethers. Exposure therapy is about becoming comfortable, little by little, with these types of situations.

As you know, CBT focuses on changes in thoughts and behaviors that result in changes in how we feel. So far, you have done a lot of work to change your thoughts, and that is absolutely awesome. Now that you have these new thoughts and core beliefs, as well as an awareness of how your thinking can become toxic and distorted, you're ready to start changing your behaviors.

It is important to have this foundation in better thinking and awareness of thought distortions before you begin exposure therapy. That is because, without healthy thoughts to help you face anxiety-inducing situations—even little by little—they can be very challenging. However, if you have new and beneficial thoughts to help replace the old thoughts that fostered your anxiety, you will be prepared to take on new situations with more confidence.

One thing to keep in mind is that exposure therapy, like changing core beliefs, takes time. It is never about going from zero to one hundred and diving straight into the deep end when the kiddie pool makes you nervous. Instead, it's about baby steps that slowly take you farther and farther outside your comfort zone and closer to your goal behavior.

If you take the time to use it properly, exposure therapy is extremely effective. It is not only used in CBT to help ease social anxiety, but is even used to treat phobias. People with these extreme fears benefit from the same basic process of exposure therapy that you will be using. That process has different specifics for every anxiety and phobia, but the steps remain the same.

Stepping Outside Your Comfort Zone

The process of exposure therapy is simply to take very small steps to work toward engaging fully in behavior that has caused you anxiety in the past. This behavior that once caused anxiety, but that you want to engage in, is called a goal behavior. Exposure therapy means no longer avoiding, entirely, the things that cause you anxiety and make you uncomfortable.

This sounds difficult. It may even be overwhelming. But, you can make a plan and follow through with it. There are a series of repeated steps for exposure therapy. This chapter will guide you through using those steps to make and implement your plan.

First, pick a goal behavior. During my first time trying exposure therapy, my goal behavior was to go to a big end-of-year party on campus. Your goal can be doing anything that makes you anxious, but is safe, and that you would like to be able to do comfortably. Because each person and their specific social anxiety is unique, your goal behavior will be unique to you.

This goal was something I would have immediately run away from, possibly literally, if I had tried it at the start. Exposure therapy is all about little steps, but we start with a big end goal in mind. This big goal helps you to determine what type of steps will be most helpful to take along the way. It will also give you an idea of how far you have to go, or how many steps you might need to take, based on how anxious the goal behavior makes you feel right now.

- Define your goal behavior. Pick an activity or behavior you would like to engage in comfortably, and write it here. This is the end goal, not the first step, so don't worry if you feel unable to try this behavior right away. You will be building up to it. Some examples are: going out with friends, attending a party, or going to the movies by yourself.

Goal behavior:

_____

_____

Second, choose a series of small steps that will make you somewhat anxious, but are less intense or anxiety-inducing than your goal behavior. I chose to accept an invitation to lunch with my roommate. Then, when she invited me to the movies with some girls from my dorm a couple of weeks later, I accepted. The next step for me was actually attending that outing. Next, I decided to try a bigger outing and signed up for a campus trip to a museum I was interested in. I kept doing similar things, over and over, until I actually felt only mildly nervous going to the big party I wanted to attend at the end of the year.

As you can see, I started small. I didn't go to a group outing first, or even second. Instead, I went to lunch with my roommate three or four times to get comfortable with new social situations. When I felt comfortable doing that, I then decided to move on to doing things with a small group. Finally, I went out with a larger group of people I didn't even know. Eventually, I was comfortable going to a party where there were lots of people I had never met.

These incremental steps toward your goal take time, but it is important not to push yourself too far too fast. If you do, it is possible that you will have a very bad experience that could even, temporarily, increase your anxiety. Make sure you choose steps that make you a bit anxious, but don't overwhelm you. Repeat a step as many times as you need, to feel more comfortable with it. Take the time you need, to gain confidence in each new situation.

The key to exposure therapy is repetition. One time might not be enough to lessen social anxiety in certain situations, but it will be enough to give you the confidence that you can try again. And, you can keep trying. Each time a step becomes comfortable enough, step it up and move to the next activity.

- Make a plan. Exposure therapy is a series of small, incremental steps. Think about what you can do that is similar to the goal behavior in some way, but causes you less anxiety. Don't worry if you feel you need to take multiple steps between where you are now and your goal. That is actually ideal, as exposure therapy will reduce anxiety more and more each time you do it.

My Plan:

_____
_____
_____

The third step in exposure therapy is to reflect. Journal—or at least think about—what went well, what could have gone better, and how you felt during the event. You must be honest about your feelings when you reflect on your experience. If you were terrified, that's okay. Maybe that means you need to try a smaller step first. If you felt anxious, but got through it, that's great! Analyze how you can keep repeating your steps and moving toward your goal.

Whether you feel like your first trial with exposure therapy went wonderfully, terribly, or somewhere in between, it is important to reflect. This reflection not only helps you gather the information that can make your next trial go better, but it also helps you build confidence. Keep your reflection realistic and undistorted.

If your emotions are running high immediately after you try exposure therapy, it is okay to wait several hours (or even a day) before you reflect. This may be more beneficial, because it will give you the chance to do your analysis with a clear mind and additional observational distance from the situation.

- Now you know the steps of exposure therapy and are ready to use your plan. Take the first step in your plan. Do a small thing that makes you uncomfortable or that you tend to avoid because of anxiety.

My first step:

_____
_____

Remember to watch for distorted thinking in these new situations. Distorted thinking can increase your social anxiety and make exposure therapy more difficult. Naturally, old automatic negative thoughts and distortions will come up, but make sure to be vigilant. When your thinking gets distorted, correct it and find more realistic thoughts to focus on instead of the distorted ones.

The final step of exposure therapy is to reward yourself, in some way, for doing a difficult but, ultimately, very good for you "thing." This can be by buying yourself a small something, treating yourself to a fancy coffee, or just taking some personal time to relax. Rewarding yourself is key because it helps to reinforce the immediate value of stepping out of your comfort zone. It is also an excellent way to show yourself some love and practice self-compassion.

Even if you didn't make it all the way through your trial, or if you feel like you didn't do it "right," it is important to reward yourself. The hardest part of exposure therapy is often just trying to do the steps. If you made any kind of genuine effort, no matter how small, you deserve a reward. Remember that you are stepping forward into change so you can know what it's like to win, and that can be a very difficult thing to do.

- Reflect on your first step. Answer the following questions about how your first attempt at exposure therapy went. If you want to go deeper, continue your reflection in your journal. Write about how you felt before, during, and after the event. Did it get easier? Was it as uncomfortable as you had expected? What could you try for your next step?

What went well:

_____
_____
_____

What didn't:

_____
_____
_____

Something to do differently:

_____
_____
_____

Before I started, I felt:

_____
_____
_____

During exposure therapy, I felt:

_____
_____
_____

Afterward, I felt:

_____
_____
_____

My reward:

_____
_____
_____

Though exposure therapy takes time, the payoffs can be immense. By properly utilizing exposure therapy in the way this workbook has walked you through it, you can build up your confidence. It is possible to become comfortable and even start to enjoy doing things that once caused you anxiety.

I'm living proof. Not only did I go to the end-of-year party on campus, but I also formed a close friendship with the young woman who invited me to it, back at the start of the semester. We still keep in touch, and neither of us can believe how much we've grown over the years. For me, a large part of that growth was jump-started by exposure therapy.

- Keep going. Continue to take small steps until you can face your goal behavior with a manageable amount of anxiety. Remember to reward yourself and reflect after each step you try.

My next step:

_____
_____
_____

As you build confidence with exposure therapy, you will begin to feel higher self-esteem and more self-love. Now that you're overcoming some of your social anxiety, it's a good time to look at other sources of self-love. The more you love yourself, the easier it is to be comfortable in any situation.

Takeaways

- Exposure therapy is one of the behavioral parts of cognitive behavioral therapy.

- It is a proven therapy process that not only reduces social anxiety, but can even help alleviate phobias.

- Before you begin exposure therapy, start with a goal behavior you want to engage in. Then, create a series of steps that challenge you to move closer to that goal behavior.

- Begin by slowly engaging in activities that once caused you anxiety and led to avoidance behavior.

- After each attempt at exposure therapy, be sure to take time to both reflect and reward yourself.

- Start small to avoid overwhelming yourself. You can work up to your goal behavior and take on bigger challenges, over time.

- Repetition is key. Only move on to the next step when you feel confident you can handle it.

- Use your new core beliefs and awareness of distorted thinking to support you as you step outside of your comfort zone with exposure therapy.

In the next chapter, we'll talk about values, and discuss how knowing ourselves and living in line with our values helps us to love ourselves more fully. We'll also look at how to face criticism, and how we can stick to our values and continue to love ourselves even when we encounter the negative opinions of others.

Chapter 7:

Understanding What Matters—Discovering Your Values and Facing Criticism

When your values are clear to you, making decisions becomes easier. —Roy E. Disney

Easier decision-making is just one of the many benefits of having clearly defined your values for yourself. It also helps you to live in accordance with those values, and to be more satisfied with your life, your actions, and yourself. This satisfaction that results from living in line with your values supports real, healthy self-love. That kind of strong self-love helps to alleviate anxiety in general, particularly in social situations.

As you encounter more social situations, you will inevitably face criticism and feedback. This can be difficult, but if you know and live by your own values, you will have the self-love and confidence required to hear the opinions of others without letting them sway your own. This chapter will give you additional tools to deal with feedback, criticism, and the anxiety they cause.

The exercises in this chapter are designed to help you identify your values. You will prioritize them for yourself, so you will know what to do when you find two values that might be competing for your time. You will also do some role-playing, to prepare for a situation where you might be criticized, and bolster your confidence to handle those types of situations.

Knowing your values and facing criticism may seem like two very different things. They are related, when it comes to self-love and self-confidence, however. The goal of all the exercises in this chapter is to be able to stay strong within yourself, and hold onto your values and what is important to you. You can use your values to draw strength from and support yourself when you feel uncomfortable with feedback, or even when you face harsh criticism.

What Are Core Values?

Core values are the things that mean the most to us. They are the principles and ways of living and behaving that we hold dear. Our values are the things we would like to make the most important in our lives and our decision-making. That being said, many people do not even have a clear grasp of their values.

The reason people often don't really know, or have labels for, their values is the same as the reason they don't know, or have words for, their core beliefs. Values are often formed early on, and usually go unexamined. It is common to know some of your values, like honesty and fairness, but to be able to name them all or prioritize them is not as common.

It may seem callous to prioritize values, but it is not. It is actually practical and helpful. We can value many things, but not everything can be the most important thing to us. Just as you can only really have one most important task on your to-do list, you can only really have one value that is actually the most important. The others will all rank somewhere behind it.

For example, you may say that family is important to you. But, how important is it? Do you make everyday decisions that support spending quality time with your family? Or, when asked to work late, do you always accept, even when you had plans to have dinner with your family that night? There's nothing wrong with choosing to put in extra time at work; but, in this scenario, it competes with family time. Having prioritized values will help you make a choice you can feel good about. Which is more important to you: career or family?

Maybe, helping others is something you consider a value. But, do you make time to volunteer or help those in need? If you do, that's great. If you don't regularly engage in those activities, think about whether you would like to take more action to support this value, or whether it may simply be a lower priority value for you. Whatever the answer is, that is okay. The most important aspect of knowing and prioritizing your values is self-honesty.

It is crucial not only to know and prioritize your values, but to act on that knowledge. Once you have clearly defined your values for yourself, you must then make conscious choices that support those values. If you do, your self-love and life satisfaction will blossom.

Whenever I have a friend who is feeling dissatisfied with their life, or unhappy without a clear reason, I recommend they look at their core values. This is because knowing and living in line with your values makes such a huge impact on your behaviors. And, as CBT teaches us, those behaviors will influence what you think and how you feel.

- List your top five personal values. These can be anything that matters deeply to you, and that you want to be a priority in your life and decision-making. My top five values are faith, family, friends, personal growth, and helping others. If you struggle to come up with ideas, take a look online. There are lots of CBT lists of values that might resonate with you.

My top five values:

_____
_____
_____
_____

- Now pick your top three values. Circle them, and then write them here, in order of importance. Do not feel any guilt about what your values are or how you prioritize them. Values are about how you live your own life and what makes you feel good about your life.

  If it helps, you might like to write these in a note on your phone, or an index card in your wallet or bag. That way, you can always keep your values close, mentally and physically.

Value #1:_____

Value #2:_____

Value #3:_____

How Identifying Values Supports Self-Love

By identifying your values, you can make choices that support those values. It is easy to be swayed, when you don't have a clear outline of your core values. But, if you know that, for example, your top value is family time, then it is harder to be pressured into staying late at work when you don't really need to. On the other hand, if you value your career advancement, you may be more likely to put in some extra hours instead of going to the bar with friends.

Two common traps of not knowing and sticking to your values are people pleasing and acting in the moment. Neither are things you should feel bad about. Everyone does a bit of both sometimes. The key is that, as default behaviors, they damage self-esteem and do not foster self-love.

People pleasing is the act of pleasing others by doing, saying, or presenting yourself the way you think they would like you to. This is easy to do when you are socially anxious and worry about what others think of you. But, it can lead to acting against your values and making choices that, even if they aren't harmful, you ultimately regret or think better of. Knowing, and sticking to, your values help you to do what will please yourself in the long term, rather than what will please others.

Acting in the moment occurs when you make choices based only on short-term goals or feelings. This kind of thinking can make you feel good temporarily, but like people pleasing, it often leads to long-term regret and can work against larger goals. Knowing your values and keeping them in mind will help you to consciously make decisions that support long-term goals rather than short-term feelings.

Making choices that fall in line with your values, instead of people pleasing or doing only what you feel in the moment, will lead to greater life satisfaction and self-love. Values support self-love because they let us live in a way we can be proud of. If we feel proud of our choices and confident in our reasons behind them, we are more able to love ourselves and see ourselves in a positive light. We are also more likely to reach our long-term goals, which are usually born out of regularly acting in line with our values.

When you act in ways that don't support your values, you feel disappointed in yourself and may even feel shame or guilt. Knowing your values clearly, as you will after you have completed the exercises in this chapter, will keep you from acting impulsively or putting others' wants before your own values. You can only live a life shaped around your values if you have a clear idea of what those values are, and what priority each holds for you.

Remember not to judge your values, and to answer all the exercises in this chapter honestly. Society, and those around us, may indeed value all sorts of different things. But the only way to feel the self-love and confidence that comes from living in line with your values is to know *your* values. This means that, even if you think you may be judged for it, you must be honest with yourself.

If you don't put a high priority on your career, even though those around you do, that's okay. It is only important that you know *your* values, and respect the difference in values others may have. People who respect your values will come to you, and those that don't can be gracefully avoided as much as possible. Never let anyone make you feel guilty for what you hold dear. Your values are yours; and, you should trust yourself, not others, to determine what those values are.

At the same time, you shouldn't seek to impose your values on others. It will cause stress for you, possibly strain your relationship, and ultimately get you nowhere. If someone is living in a way that you do not approve of, you do have choices. You can accept it as a fact that some people will hold different values than you, or you can choose to stop spending time with someone who holds values that counter your own. Either way, you are free to choose whether to continue or end the relationship.

Once you understand what your values are, it is important to begin asking why they matter to you. Knowing your *why* for values, like knowing your reason for doing anything, will increase your motivation to live in line with those values. Your *why* is important because reason supports action. We are much more likely to do, and continue doing, things when we understand why they are important. Living our values is no different.

- Knowing your reasons is very important. Why is each value a priority for you? What does it mean to you? How are you currently making, or not making, it a priority in your life? Is there anything you would like to change to live more in line with this value? Write your answers here and continue your exploration in your journal, if you want to dig deeper.

Why value 1 is important:

_____
_____
_____

Why value 2 is important:

_____
_____
_____

Why value 3 is important:

_____
_____
_____

Let's take a look at an example of how values clarification—the CBT term for the work we've been doing in this chapter—can lead to greater self-love and life satisfaction. We'll examine the case of a woman named Meredith, whom I learned about in my research.

Meredith was a hard-working mother of two, who found herself unhappy and lacking in self-esteem after her youngest son left for college. She felt unsure of herself, and decision-making became difficult for the first time in her life. Meredith's dissatisfaction grew until she sought out a book on CBT. She wasn't really sure what was going on, but she wanted to find answers and help herself out of the rut she was quickly falling into.

When she learned about core values, she began to understand the root of her problem. Meredith was feeling lost because she had always put being a supportive mother as her top value in life. Now that her children were both out of the house, she continued to be a loving mother, but they didn't need her on a daily basis. This left her unsure of what to do in the time she would usually have spent caring for, and enjoying being with, her sons.

Meredith had never thought about, or analyzed, her values before. Now was an important time to do so. Even if we have great and strongly held values, major shifts and life changes can cause those values to change. This doesn't make you a bad person, or make you less strong in your values. It didn't mean any of those things about Meredith. It simply means that circumstances have changed so much that one value may not need as much attention, or that something else may become more important.

In addition to Meredith's example, consider how a new baby reorders the priorities of its parents, or how a new job may make you focus more closely on your career. It is natural that these types of life changes can shake up your values. So, when you undergo a major life change, it can be helpful to redo these values clarification exercises and see what the results are.

Meredith decided to redefine her values after her life change. Being a good mother was still at the top of her list, but after some soul-searching, she realized she also highly valued creativity. This was not a huge surprise, as she had been an avid painter before her children were born, and still spent time making the occasional sketch or drawing.

Meredith was now free to devote a lot more time to her second-highest value of creativity. She even decided to turn one of her spare rooms into an art studio and took up painting again. These steps were possible because Meredith had taken the time to clarify and prioritize her values, and to analyze where she most valued focusing her new free time and energy.

By acting on this value she had previously had little time for, Meredith found a new joy and confidence. Choices became easier, and she started to feel more fulfilled. Her self-love and confidence bounced back and grew with each new painting. No longer did she worry about what to do with her spare time; instead, she painted and drew in her sketchbook. These activities helped Meredith to live in accordance with her values and to find happiness, after feeling adrift when a life change required her to clarify her values.

Identifying values is the first step. The second step is to act on those values, just like Meredith did. Values can be helpful, even if they remain in the realm of thought, but they are most useful for building self-love and confidence when you put them into action.

- Think of an activity that supports each of your top three values. It can be something you already do, or it can be something you want to start doing. List these activities here and make a plan to engage in each one at least once in the next two weeks.

To support value 1, I will:

_____
_____
_____

To support value 2, I will:

_____
_____
_____

To support value 3, I will:

_____
_____
_____

As you put your values into action and take part in activities that support them, you are eventually going to face feedback and even criticism. These are natural parts of working with others, but they can be very anxiety-inducing. In the next section, we'll look at how to face these kinds of social situations, and still stick up for yourself and remain true to your values.

Staying True to Your Values

As you begin to encounter more social situations and make more choices concerning your values, you will eventually face feedback, and even criticism. This can be tough. A large part of many people's social anxiety, including my own, results from a fear of judgment and criticism. There are ways you can make it easier to deal with, though. We'll look at a few of those strategies in this section.

Values clarification can be one step toward being better able to handle criticism and feedback. When you know your own values, and are confident you are living a life that supports them, then you are naturally more resilient to the impacts of criticism.

One of the best strategies for dealing with uncomfortable feedback, or even harsh criticism, is to prepare ahead of time. Role-playing out a possible scenario can really help here. Using role-playing to prepare for criticism takes only two repeated steps. Before you begin, think about the situation where you are concerned about facing criticism.

- Describe a coming situation where you might face criticism or feedback. It can be an official type of criticism, like a performance review or getting a grade on a paper; or, it could be unofficial feedback, like presenting your ideas at a committee meeting or helping to plan a group activity.

My situation:

_____
_____
_____

Once you have clearly described the situation, consider what you might hear from the other person, or people, involved. You can do this in your own mind, or you can role-play in real time and ask a trusted friend or therapist (if you've chosen to work with one) to play the part of the person who will be giving you feedback. Practice responses to various possible criticisms. You can consider the most likely and, if you are feeling up to it, the most negative or possibly the "worst" criticism, as well.

Be aware that, as you do this exercise, it can become emotional, especially if you are highly sensitive to criticism. That's okay. Take a break and step back, if needed. The goal of this kind of role-playing is to prepare in a way that reduces the emotional intensity of the criticism when you actually hear it. One way to do that is to feel the associated emotions ahead of time to lessen their severity.

When you role-play a possibly critical situation, don't worry too much about capturing exactly what the other person might say word-for-word. Emphasize themes and types of criticism to prepare for. It is very difficult to know exactly what someone might say, but it is much easier to guess what topics they might speak about.

On the other hand, if certain language is triggering for you, it might be a good idea to prepare for that. Think about any words or phrases that really sting or hurt. Don't consider things that are purely nasty, like slurs; these shouldn't be said, and if you think they will be, it may be best to avoid the situation altogether. Instead, focus on things that hurt you, but others might not be bothered by as much.

For example, I am very sensitive to the word *weird*. My mother, in the past, used it as a euphemism for "socially unacceptable or awkward." My mother would say, "Stop acting so weird, Franceene." Although I know she meant to encourage me to behave differently, it stung. My friend Erin thinks *weird* is a great compliment, however. She loves off-beat movies and unusual art. She might say something like "Bjork's music is great. But, her videos are so weird!" These are the kinds of words you might want to be aware of for yourself, and prepare for.

- List a few possible criticisms or feedback you might hear from the person, or people, in the situation you described above. Try to focus more on content than the specific language they might use. If you know that specific language can be very triggering for you, then do try to prepare for that possibility.

Most likely possible criticism:

_____
_____
_____

Most anxiety-inducing possible criticism:

_____
_____
_____

Other possible criticisms:

_____
_____
_____

Now, think about how you can calmly and assertively respond to that criticism. Communicating assertively means speaking in a calm, even tone; not interrupting others; and being willing to compromise without giving up all of your wants and needs. Assertiveness is a key communication skill that benefits both parties. You will feel more confident for calmly expressing your thoughts and feelings, and the other person will feel listened to and respected.

Remember to stick to your values. Do not do or say anything rash or hurtful to another person, no matter how much the criticism stung. If you feel that what they said was unduly harsh or mean, say so assertively. If emotions—yours or theirs—begin to run too high, end the conversation and excuse yourself, rather than abandon assertive and respectful communication.

Also, do not betray yourself by backing down. It is good to stand up for yourself and your values. Practicing possible responses, ahead of time, will help you to stay calm when you actually face criticism and not let anxiety overwhelm you. Once you have prepared the possible criticism you want to work with, it's time to practice responses. Try to come up with a couple of assertive responses to each criticism you listed. Having a few prepared responses will help you not to be caught off guard, while also not sound as if you are speaking from a script.

- Think carefully and write out possible responses to each criticism you listed above. Remember to stay assertive and stick up for yourself, your values, and your ideas.

Response to the most likely criticism:

_____
_____
_____

Response to the most anxiety-inducing criticism:

_____
_____
_____

Response to any other possible criticism:

_____
_____
_____

Preparation is key, but there are other points to remember that can help you face criticism and feedback with grace and self-love, as well. Don't let your thinking become distorted when you get feedback. Watch for distortions in your thoughts as you hear out what others have to say. It can be hard, but it is important to take what others say as what they mean, and not overgeneralize or make negative predictions based on it.

It also helps to know that, usually, people are not giving feedback either about you as a person or about the quality of your values. Remember that feedback normally has a lot more to do with ideas or abilities, both of which can be changed—or even improved. If someone does not like your ideas or your work, it does not mean that there is anything wrong with you as a person, or even that they don't like you on a personal level.

If someone is giving harsh criticism or feedback about you as a person, or your values, it's time to stay calm and take a close look at the situation. Is this person trying to help you? For example, is it a close friend letting you know that you may have accidentally offended someone? In situations where it is a friend providing encouraging feedback that may help you grow or improve, hear them out and use your own judgment to decide what you will do with what they say.

In a situation where the person's intent is simply to be hurtful or demeaning to you, your best course of action is to excuse yourself from the situation. After you do, take time to think about if you want to continue to interact with that person, or if they may be someone best kept at a distance. If you do want to continue the relationship with the hurtful person, do so only after you have made it clear that they spoke to you inappropriately, and that you will not allow them to do so in the future.

Setting boundaries is a key act of self-love. It shows that you deserve respect and are willing to give it to yourself and make sure others give it to you. Do not be afraid to set assertive, clearly defined boundaries. It can feel uncomfortable to do so, but if you set firm boundaries, you will save yourself potential discomfort and anxiety in the future.

Growing your own confidence and self-love is another huge step toward building your resilience to criticism. If you take an honest assessment of yourself and are able to find something you like about yourself and things you know you are good at, it can be easier to hear uncomfortable or negative things from others. Building a solid foundation of self-love, that is rooted in reality, keeps your self-esteem from being as badly hurt by the opinions of others.

- Make an assessment of yourself. List four things you know you do well, or are proud of. Hold on to these four things in your mind. Use them to anchor yourself when criticism threatens your self-esteem.

Positive thing 1:

_____
_____
_____

Positive thing 2:

_____
_____
_____

Positive thing 3:

_____
_____
_____

Positive thing 4:

_____
_____
_____

You may wonder what to do if someone criticizes one of the things you think you do well. The answer is to consider their criticism, but keep in mind that, even if you are doing well, there is always room for improvement. No one is perfect at any skill, so their criticism may be accurately pointing out areas where you can improve.

If you disagree with their criticism, then that's fine. Listen to your own judgment, above all else. Know that someone may simply have different tastes than you, or may have a standard that is different from yours. That's okay. If you don't agree with a particular criticism, then let the other person have their opinion and let the matter go.

If you need to defend your work or your skills, then do so respectfully and calmly. State why you disagree with the criticism and what you think is good about your work or skill, if appropriate. Be assertive and keep your emotions in check, as you should in any communication. Always remember that your own opinion of yourself and your abilities should be the most important to you; the opinions of others can have a place in your mind, but your own thoughts should have the most sway.

Keep in mind that, no matter how much you prepare or how high your self-love is, it can be hurtful to hear criticism. This is natural, because we are all social beings who want to be liked, respected, and cared for by our peers. We want our ideas and work recognized and acknowledged. Criticism can feel like an attack. In fact, the brain processes social rejection the same way it processes physical pain.

Being anxious about criticism and feedback, or feeling hurt by it, is not only normal—but very natural. The goal of these exercises is not to entirely remove the sting of others' opinions, but to make sure that it is manageable and in proportion to the importance and type of feedback or criticism.

Takeaways

- Core values are the things that mean the most to us in life—what we consider most important.
- Getting clear about what your values are, and in what order you rank them lets you live in line with those values.

- Acting in accordance with and making choices that support your values allows you to feel good about yourself and the life you choose to live.

- Knowing your values is a key first step, but building confidence and self-love truly begins when you take actions that support your values.

- When you are going to face criticism, prepare ahead of time by role-playing the scenario and coming up with responses.

- Use self-love, compassion, and positive self-talk to help prevent criticism from damaging your self-esteem.

- Remember, it is natural to be hurt by criticism, but don't let the opinions of *others* hurt your opinion of *yourself*.

The next chapter examines how CBT encourages us to focus on the positive, while not denying the reality of our lives, which can be another helpful strategy for handling feedback. That being said, it can also be a bit of a balancing act, since evolution has programmed the human mind to focus more heavily on the negative. But, with our values in our minds, we can look at what we have to be grateful for, what is good in our lives, and also what we might strive to change.

Chapter 8:

Positivity for Change—Focusing on the Positive

Keep your face to the sunshine and you cannot see a shadow. —Helen Keller

Helen Keller paints a beautiful image of the importance of positive thinking. CBT doesn't tell us to deny the existence of shadows, but it reminds us not to focus on them so much that we exclude the sunny day around us. As we will see, our minds have evolved to focus on the negative. CBT offers us techniques—like cognitive restructuring—to balance out that innate negative thinking, and helps us view the world and our situations as realistically as possible.

The exercises in this chapter focus equally on cognitive restructuring and positive self-talk. I have found that the two work well together, and that restructuring our negative self-talk is often a good way to learn just how unrealistic our negative views of ourselves can be. With the use of cognitive restructuring and positive self-talk, you will have two new tools to support your self-love.

Negative Mental Bias

Numerous psychological studies have proven that adults tend to weigh negative information, experiences, and emotions more heavily than positive ones. This means we tend to think of negative things as being more important, meaningful, or "real" than positive things. In some cases, we even have a more accurate and vivid memory of negative events than of positive ones.

This can cloud our perception of our lives and the world, and lead us down a path of negativity. I also often see negativity and pessimism lauded as being more "realistic." The truth is that an overly negative view of the world is just as unrealistic and damaging as an overly optimistic one. To use a familiar metaphor, the glass is actually both half empty and half full. We need to acknowledge both the good and the bad to build an accurate impression of our lives.

It may seem odd that we have such a strong negative bias in our minds when it is, in fact, a bias that creates a distorted worldview. The reason for our negative bias may be evolutionary. One current theory suggests that if we more heavily weigh and more vividly recall negative experiences, we will be more risk averse.

This risk aversion was great for our ancestors. Ancient humans needed to do everything they could to stay safe, healthy, and pain-free. What can be easily healed today could have been a life-ending injury or illness even a few centuries ago. By more vividly recalling negative events, our ancestors were less likely to repeat their mistakes and more likely to learn from them.

In our modern world, we face different challenges. Although most of our daily stressors are not life or death, our brains still interpret many of them as such. Our brains also still have the negative bias that we gained from our evolutionary ancestors. This can lead to a lot of stress. Sometimes, that stress is over things that are not dangerous or life-threatening at all.

Group alienation is a good example of an evolutionary stressor that no longer carries the same dangers. Previously, being an outcast from the social group greatly decreased a person's chances of survival and cut them off from sources of food, shelter, and protection. Today, being socially ostracized rarely has any life-threatening consequences in our daily lives, but our minds still focus on it and worry about it as if it were a matter of life and death.

If we also consider the negative mental bias we have, it can be easy to see how social anxiety can arise. These fears are very real, and our minds do not understand—on a biological level—that they do not represent a threat to our safety. This leads to a lot of stress and anxiety over situations that, in modern times, are not life-threatening or even physically dangerous. This stress is experienced by the body as a real and immediate danger.

We still experience these stresses so intensely because evolution hasn't caught up to our safer way of life yet. Our brains are still stuck in a world of life-or-death consequences. Because of that, they create stress for us that is detrimental to our mental and physical health.

But, we can use CBT tools, rational thinking, and other modern skills to overcome our negative mental bias and balance our view of situations, to reduce our social anxiety and other stressors. By reframing and focusing a bit more on the positive, our lives can seem brighter and our view of the world actually becomes less distorted by the negative bias in the mind.

- Record some of your negative thoughts and see if they are realistic. We all have negative thoughts, and sometimes those thoughts are warranted. However, they are often the result of negative mental bias. Even if you cannot label a thought with a specific thinking distortion, it may still be unrealistic. Check three negative thoughts against the objective facts associated with them.

Negative thought:

_____
_____

The facts:

_____
_____

Is it realistic?:_____

Negative thought:

_____
_____

The facts:

_____
_____

Is it realistic?:_____

Negative thought:

_____
_____

The facts:

_____

_____

Is it realistic?:_____

Looking at the Positive

CBT doesn't recommend that you simply "think positive" or "look on the bright side." Positive thinking alone can actually be dangerous! It can lead you to deny the reality of a situation, or to repress important and helpful, albeit uncomfortable, emotions that are pointing at problems in your life. CBT always emphasizes looking at things realistically. And, that means being neither too negative nor too positive about a situation.

In CBT terms, positive thinking is often used to create balanced thoughts. This technique is called cognitive restructuring, meaning that it focuses on restructuring your thinking. To use cognitive restructuring, first identify a negative thought about yourself, someone else, or a situation. Once you have identified a negative thought, weigh it against the facts. Does your view seem realistic, when compared with what you know is objectively true?

If it does, then you need to try problem-solving on your own (covered in the next chapter) or seek help from an outside source. It is entirely possible that a negative thought is realistic. It could be pointing you toward a circumstance or situation that is a problem that requires solving. In that case, do not discount the negative thoughts and try to cheer up.

Instead, be proactive and take a look at what you can do to make a change. This type of active solution-seeking for your problems will do more for you than simply trying to think positively. In a situation where negativity fits the facts, the best way to begin feeling better is to take active steps toward resolving the situation.

If the negative thought does not fit the facts of the situation, then it's time to try cognitive restructuring. To engage in cognitive restructuring, first take your negative thought and rework it into its positive opposite. The opposite thought must be wholly positive. It doesn't have to be realistic. The next step is where you bring your thinking back to the realistic balance point, by combining the negative and positive thoughts to create a new, accurate thought.

My friend Ann often found herself thinking: *I do everything wrong. I am such a screw-up*. I heard her say or mumble things similar to this on several occasions. When she was feeling very down on herself for a perceived mistake one day, I suggested she try cognitive restructuring. Ann took her negative thought and restructured it to its most positive opposite. She thought: *I do everything right. I never make mistakes*.

Notice that it is not important, in the second step of cognitive restructuring, that you think of a realistic thought. This overly positive thought is just a stepping stone, so it is okay if you realize that it is unrealistic. The important thing in step two is that you frame things as positively as you possibly can. In some cases, it can help you realize how unrealistic your negative thought is, when you realize that its exact opposite is also unrealistic.

Now, you merge the two thoughts. You look at the negative and positive thoughts, and come up with a new, balanced thought that accurately fits the situation in question. For Ann, this new thought was: *I make some mistakes, but I also do many things right every day.* This new thought is balanced and, undeniably, more realistic than the thought that she never did anything right.

- Circle any of your negative thoughts from the first exercise that doesn't fit the facts. Find the opposite, positive thought. Then, blend the two with cognitive restructuring to create a balanced thought that acknowledges any real negatives, while also not denying any real positives.

Negative thought:

_____
_____

Positive thought:

_____
_____

Balanced thought:

_____
_____

Negative thought:

_____
_____

Positive thought:

_____
_____

Balanced thought:

_____
_____

Negative thought:

_____
_____

Positive thought:

_____
_____

Balanced thought:

_____
_____

Another technique that emphasizes acknowledging the positive is listing the pros and cons. This is a simple exercise, but there are some rules. First, you must always find at least one pro. Second, you must be honest and objective. Do not try to make a pros and cons list about a situation when you are highly emotional. If you do, it is likely to be inaccurate.

Instead, wait until you have some distance from a situation. Once you have the necessary mental distance from a situation, it can be a good idea to make a pros and cons list. These types of lists help you to see what might be good in a bad situation, or at least aspects of it that are in your favor. To make a pros and cons list, just list all of the positive aspects of a situation and all of the negative aspects of the situation. Try your best to make it at least balanced, but know that it is realistic that some situations will be more negative than positive.

- Try this role-playing exercise. Think about an upcoming difficult situation. It could be something you have to do, that you don't want to do, or maybe something stressful that might happen. If you can't think of something from your life, use an example from a favorite book or movie. Pretend you are facing a problem faced by one of the characters. Make a list of the positive and negative aspects of the situation. Think hard. Notice that, even in a tough scenario, it is possible to find some good points, or at least an opportunity for change or growth that exists alongside the negatives. When you are done with your lists, write a balanced view of the situation.

Positives:

_____
_____

Negatives:

_____
_____

Balanced view:

_____

_____

Ann's story also brings up another key element of CBT: self-talk. Self-talk is simply the things we think about and say to ourselves. Self-talk is instrumental in forming a positive relationship with ourselves and loving ourselves. You can't truly love someone if you always say hurtful or negative things to them. The same is true for loving yourself.

When we engage in negative self-talk, we damage our self-esteem. This prevents us from loving ourselves, and also leads to more social anxiety. If we aren't treating and speaking to ourselves in loving ways, it is hard to anticipate others will treat us differently. This feeds social anxiety and distrust of others.

Another drawback of negative self-talk is that we shape our worldview with the things we tell ourselves. Confirmation bias is the tendency of the mind to seek out and retain information that supports what we already believe to be true. When we believe negative things about ourselves, we get stuck in a cycle. Confirmation bias leads us to see more and more reasons to think negatively about ourselves.

On the other hand, when we speak to ourselves in ways that are realistic, balanced, and encouraging, we engage in a radical act of self-love. This type of self-talk needs to be balanced, even if we emphasize being gentle with ourselves. Unrealistically positive views of ourselves can be damaging in other ways.

As you begin to engage in positive self-talk, you'll learn that confirmation bias can also work in your favor. By creating a mindset where you look for confirmation that you have positive qualities and skills, you will create a positive cycle where you see more evidence for that view of yourself. Your mind seeks out and focuses on information that supports your self-talk and makes you seem right, so positive self-talk actually leads to more positive thinking.

- Engage in positive self-talk. If you catch yourself speaking negatively to or about yourself, stop. Pause and take a breath. Then, say something positive about yourself. It may not be related directly to your negative thoughts. That's okay. Any positive self-talk will help to balance your thinking, so you are not always chipping away at your self-esteem without building yourself back up. Fill out this list with some positive things you can say about yourself.

I like myself because:

_____

_____

I am good at:

I am beautiful because:

_____
_____

I am proud of myself for:

_____
_____

I help others by:

_____
_____

Something else good about me:

_____
_____

Loving and kind self-talk may feel strange to you, especially if you spent many years speaking negatively toward yourself. Talk to yourself the way you would a valued friend or family member. You don't have to ignore the things you want to change or improve, but don't beat yourself up. Instead, remain encouraging and remind yourself of the things you already do well. If you find yourself being too negative with yourself, remember to try cognitive restructuring of your negative thoughts and self-talk. And, when a situation is what's getting you down, try making a balanced pros and cons list, so you can see what good might be there that you didn't notice before.

Takeaways

- All humans have an innate negative mental bias. This causes us to think that the negative information outweighs positive information, even when that is not truly the case.

- CBT encourages positive thinking, not for its own sake, but to balance this negative bias in our minds.

- Cognitive restructuring is the process of thinking of the opposite, positive version of a negative thought, and then balancing those two thoughts into a realistic thought.

- Another method to look for, and focus on, the positives is a pros and cons list. Make these objectively, and always try to find at least one positive. Strive to keep your lists balanced or with more positives. This won't always be possible, but it's a good goal.

- Self-talk impacts not only how we feel about ourselves, but also social anxiety. Because of this, it is important we speak to ourselves in encouraging, realistic ways. We should make sure our self-talk balances both our positive qualities and the qualities we would like to change in ourselves.

In the following chapter, we will look at what to do when changing your thinking isn't enough. Sometimes, we face real problems that we need to take action on. Denying the need to take action in these circumstances won't get you anywhere. CBT encourages us to take an active role in changing our lives. With the help of CBT's straightforward methods, you can begin to solve the problems you face and make real changes.

Chapter 9:

Rise to the Challenge—Problem Solving With CBT

We cannot solve our problems with the same level of thinking that created them. —Albert Einstein

The type of thinking or behavior that has caused us a problem won't be able to solve that same problem. It's a simple fact, but it begs the question. If we need to engage in new or different thinking to solve our problems, what can we do?

CBT offers us the new level of thinking we need when it comes to problem-solving. It's as easy as following the five steps that we'll discuss in this chapter. These steps are flexible and broadly applicable, so they can be used for almost any problem you could encounter.

This chapter's exercises may seem simple, but it's all about doing the work and practicing the steps of problem-solving. As Einstein said, you'll need to develop new ways of thinking to solve problems. Use the exercises in this chapter to try out thinking differently about a current problem. If you don't have any current problems, feel free to try finding a different solution to a past problem.

The Importance of Problem-Solving

We have already seen that CBT doesn't tell us that positive thinking will solve all our problems. And, we know that CBT advises us to change our thoughts and behaviors to solve problems related to how we feel. But, what steps do we take when we encounter a problem that needs a specific solution? What do we do if we can't find that solution immediately? We problem-solve, of course.

CBT encourages us to approach problems in the same way we are encouraged to think. That means a rational, balanced, and realistic view of the problem must be taken. It is fine to have feelings, even intense feelings, about a problem. But, once you have worked through how you feel and have a clearer head, it's time to start working on an active solution.

You should always deal with your feelings before you try to problem-solve. Strong emotions can cloud your thinking and make problem-solving more difficult, or cause you to settle on a solution that is not the best for you because you chose it based on emotional factors and not practical factors, such as ease of implementation or the amount of effort required.

The CBT technique for solving problems that I will teach you in this chapter may seem overly simplistic, but simplicity is part of its design. Because it is so simple, it is easily done; and, because the steps are not too specific, they can be applied to a wide range of problems. This is a big advantage, because it means once you learn this method, you are free to use it over and over again, for any problems that may arise.

The CBT Method of Problem-Solving

The first step in the CBT method of problem-solving is to clearly identify the problem. I advise writing it out. This helps you really solidify what the problem is, and to give yourself something to refer to that is free from potential emotional distortion.

Try to use language that is as unemotional as possible. Remember that the time and place to really work through and feel your emotions is not when you are problem-solving. Instead, problem-solve after the peak of your emotions about a problem has subsided. Take some time to process your feelings first, if you need to, and then you can move on to problem-solving. Try to take these steps with as clear a head as possible.

If you begin to feel you are getting too emotional while working on your problem, take a break and step back for a minute. That is why I advise problem-solving in a written form. That way, you won't forget where you were or what steps you were working on, if you decide to take a break and return to it in a little while.

The reason that you want to define the problem from a logical frame of mind is that you want to make sure you are solving the right problem. If you look too emotionally at your situation, you may cloud your idea of what is really going on, or what aspects of the situation you are in control of. Take Tracy, for instance; she has regular fights with her husband and wants to repair the relationship. They often argue over money.

If she thought from an emotional place, Tracy may have thought the problem is that: *Steven spends too much*. This could be the case, but it is not a problem for Tracy to solve. Steven's spending is not in her control. Instead, a better, more logical problem might be: *Steven and I do not agree about what to save and what to spend*. This problem is something Tracy has at least partial control over. If she looks at this problem, Tracy can have a discussion with Steven, make a family budget with him, and maybe seek a financial or marriage counselor to work on their disagreements.

There is a concept from another form of therapy known as dialectic behavioral therapy (DBT), a type of therapy based on CBT, called "wise mind." A wise mind is when our logical and emotional minds are balanced. We are not thinking too much about our emotions, but we are not denying them either. This is the state you should seek to use when you define and solve problems.

When it comes to problems, think of your emotions as signposts. You are the one in the driver's seat, and you have ultimate control over where you go in life. Your emotions are there to draw your attention to things. Maybe you are sad because you need to resolve an issue or leave a toxic situation. Maybe your anger is coming up because you need to be more assertive in your relationships. These types of emotions can inform your problem-solving, but they shouldn't be the main factor in your decision-making.

- Try it out! If you have a problem you are trying to solve, try this five-step process out for yourself. Make sure to engage in it when you are in a "wise mind," and not when you are feeling overly emotional or are entirely repressing your feelings about the situation. If the problem is very upsetting, get some space and calm down before you define the problem or generate solutions. Here is some space to work through the steps, but if you need more room, feel free to take out your journal or work on your computer.

The problem is:

_____
_____
_____
_____

Once you have the problem clearly defined and written out in as unemotional a way as possible, you're ready for step two. In step two, you come up with as many solutions to the problem as you possibly can. The goal here is not for each solution to be ideal, and at this stage, you aren't even picking a solution. You just want to generate as many ideas as possible. For obvious reasons, I call this step the "brainstorming" step.

Let's look at Ryan's example from a previous chapter. Job loss is a common issue in life and one that can be devastating, but it is also solvable. For Ryan, writing out the problem, step one may look like, "I have been let go from my job and need to figure out what I am going to do." This states the problem, but does not get into emotional language about how Ryan feels about the problem.

Now, it's time to generate some solutions. Those can range from the obvious "look for another job in the same field," to the more unusual "take some time off and travel with the money I have saved," or somewhere in between: "look for a new job in a new field I have always wanted to work in."

- Take step two and brainstorm some solutions for yourself.

Solutions:

_____
_____
_____

Each of these solutions has its own pros and cons. At this point, you are not looking to evaluate the quality of the solution. You are simply writing down everything you can think of that *qualifies* as a solution to your problem, whether it is particularly good, or even feasible.

Step three involves narrowing down your options. Pick the two or three best solutions. What *best* means is up to you. They should be solutions you feel are actually achievable, will help the problem, and appeal to you in some way. Write those two or three best solutions on the top of a page, each. Then, you are going to list the pros and cons of each one. This will help you compare your solutions and choose the single best option for you.

- Now, it's time to look at your solutions and choose what you think will be the best options. Unless one jumps out immediately, it's okay to pick two, or even three. We'll narrow it down in the next step. Remember, *best* is up to your judgment, but should include ease of implementation and level of satisfaction with the likely outcome.

Possible solutions:

_____
_____
_____

Sometimes, after brainstorming solutions, the best one will pop out at you immediately. If that happens, it's fine to skip step three and move directly to step four, using the best solution from brainstorming. However, if you want to consider a solution more closely, you can still do the pros and cons without comparing. This method of looking at a single solution helps you to see how it will benefit you in the short and long term, and what issues or struggles might arise as you try to implement it.

- List the pros and cons of each of your solutions. Here, there is space to compare two solutions, but if you have more you want to look at, simply work on your computer or in your journal.

Solution 1 Pros:

_____
_____
_____

Solution 1 Cons:

_____
_____
_____

Solution 2 Pros:

_____
_____
_____

Solution 2 Cons:

_____
_____
_____

Step four is to choose your single best solution. Look for the one that has the highest chance of creating the most desirable outcome for you. Then, put that solution into action. It may take time, and it will definitely take some work, but do your best to make this solution work, and see if you can solve the problem.

Don't get rid of your brainstormed solutions or your pros and cons list! If your first solution doesn't work, they may be helpful to refer back to, if you need to rework the same problem, or if something similar happens in the future. It is helpful to do this in your journal or to save it digitally. This way, you have your notes to refer back to as you continue to implement your solution, or in case you need to try another one.

Finally, step five is to evaluate how well your solution worked. Keep in mind what went right, what could have gone better, how closely to expectations the solution worked, and any other details. If your first solution did not work, evaluate in step five *why* it did not work. Then, go back to your brainstorming and choose a new solution to work with.

- Implement and evaluate your solution. If it takes time, feel free to come back to this chapter, or to record immediate results here and then more detailed continuing progress in your journal. Consider how well your solution worked, how difficult it might have been to implement, how it made you feel, how it impacted others, and any other details you think might be worth noting.

Results:_____
_____
_____
_____

As you can see, the CBT method for problem-solving is broadly applicable. It can be used in a wide range of circumstances. To take these steps may seem mechanical or emotionless, but there is a reason. We seek to solve problems logically, so our "emotional mind" doesn't outweigh our "rational mind."

Try these steps next time you have a problem to solve and see if they help. At the least, they will get you started off on the right foot. Once you're moving in the right direction, you can get your problem solved, and then evaluate the solution and the problem-solving steps, so you can do better if you ever face the same or a similar problem.

For more practice, you can even tell a friend. If a friend comes to me with a problem or is in need of advice, I often suggest they try this method of problem-solving. I'll even offer to help them work through it. It can be important just to hear others out sometimes, but if they want a solution, sharing this technique is a great way to help someone help themselves. Plus, it will give you more practice in CBT problem-solving, too. Working with trusted friends on problems can also help, because one of you may think of a solution that never would have occurred to the other person.

Another, more playful, way to practice is to role-play different situations. It can be entertaining to take a character's problem from a book or movie and apply these steps. See if you can come up with a different solution, maybe one that even leads to a happier ending. This may seem silly, but it is a good way to practice CBT skills so that you have them at your fingertips when a serious time arises, and you really need them for yourself.

- Try role-playing a problem from a favorite book or movie. See if you can't arrive at a happier ending for the characters!

The problem:

_____
_____
_____

Character's solution:

_____
_____
_____

My Solutions:
_____
_____
_____

Best solution:
_____
_____
_____

Pros:
_____
_____
_____

Cons:
_____
_____
_____

How it might work out:
_____
_____
_____

Takeaways

- CBT can be used to solve problems and find solutions. It uses a five-step method to do this.

- Remember to problem-solve from a place of wise mind. This means balancing your logic and emotions, to come up with a solution that will be logically useful and as personally satisfying as possible.

- The five steps seem simple, but they are designed to be applicable to any problem, and to help you solve problems in a balanced and rational way.

- The steps of CBT problem-solving are:

    o Identify the problem.

    o Brainstorm solutions.

    o Pick the best few by weighing the pros and cons.

    o Implement your best solution.

    o Evaluate how your solution worked, and reflect on the outcomes.

Life isn't all about solving problems, though. It is even better when we can be proactive and move toward goals of our own choosing. In our final chapter, we will talk about setting goals the CBT way, so that we can reach new heights and better our lives.

Chapter 10:

New Horizons—Setting Goals the CBT Way

Setting goals is the first step to turning the invisible into the visible. —Tony Robbins

Tony Robbins has inspired millions of people to work toward their goals. His definition of goals as a first step is very insightful. Without goals, we cannot achieve our dreams, or even know what dreams we are reaching for. But, it is true that, with goals, we can make things that were once invisible into real parts of our daily lives. This chapter looks at how to set goals with CBT, so you can move forward and continue your journey toward self-love and freedom from social anxiety.

These exercises will help you to set a goal for yourself and begin tracking your progress toward it. Think about anything that you think you can achieve that would support you as you continue your journey toward greater self-esteem and freedom from social anxiety and toxic thinking.

The Importance of Goals

We all need to set goals to continually improve ourselves and our lives. Goals also help us to stay on the right path and maintain the gains we have earned up to this point. Setting a goal to continue something, or not to go back to an old way of being, is just as valid as setting a goal to achieve a new milestone. Always have a clear goal in mind, but never feel bad if that goal is simply to continue with the progress you have already made. You don't have to constantly be striving if you are currently happy with your life.

Goals give us something to work toward and help us build our self-esteem, by showing us that we can achieve the things we desire if we work hard. However, unachieved—or worse, unachievable—goals, can set us up for failure, which will damage our self-esteem and erode the gains we have made toward greater self-love.

CBT teaches us how to set goals that are more easily achieved, because they are very realistic and attainable in the first place. The acronym for CBT's method of goal setting is also used in other forms of therapy, and sometimes in the corporate world: SMART goals. SMART goals are, in fact, smart because they are designed to be more attainable from the beginning than the unstructured types of goals people often set for themselves.

SMART goals have a built-in plan for success and keep us focused on not only what we want to achieve, but how we can effectively achieve it. This built-in plan and timing, that is part of a SMART goal, is a large reason why they have become so popular in therapy and other avenues of life, as well.

Like CBT's problem-solving method, the steps for setting a SMART goal are designed to be applicable to a wide range of goals. The specific goal isn't important, and anything you want to achieve can be formulated as a SMART goal, or a series of SMART goals, if it needs to be broken down into smaller steps. Large goals are great, but remember that, sometimes, we need to take smaller steps and move along a path to reach our desired destination.

Start to think of a goal—whether that's something you'd like to work toward, or something you've already got that you want to maintain. We'll look at the steps for setting SMART goals, and why they benefit self-esteem and set you up for success, in the next section.

Setting SMART Goals

SMART stands for *specific*, *measurable*, *attainable*, *realistic*, and *time-bound*. The order may seem odd. Frankly, I think that *attainable* and *realistic* should come after *specific*, but SMART goals are easier to remember. The steps work in any order. So, if it helps you to mix them up, that's fine. SMART goals are a planning strategy, so you don't have to adhere to the order of steps as long as you follow them all. For ease, I'll explain the steps of SMART, in order.

Specific means that a goal is specifically defined. My last goal was to lose weight. This is not a specific goal. It is not possible to say I have achieved it, because I can technically always lose more weight. At the same time, if I wanted to, it is also easy to stop because losing even a single pound counts as losing weight.

A specific version of the goal to lose weight would be to lose ten pounds. This is a very specific goal. It is easy to tell exactly when you have achieved it, and you know exactly what you are working toward.

- Set a SMART goal for yourself. Use the advice in this chapter to set a SMART goal. Think about what you would like to accomplish. It may be something that you can do by continuing to apply the techniques you've learned in this workbook, or it could be something completely different. Just make sure it fits the criteria of a SMART goal.

Specific goal:

_____
_____

The second step to setting a SMART goal is to make sure it is measurable. For weight loss, this is relatively easy. You can measure your progress on a scale. For other goals, this might require getting creative. I have a friend who wants to write a novel. To make his goal measurable, he decided he would get in a certain amount of writing hours a week. He times each writing session and keeps those times in his planner. At the end of the week, he adds them up to see if he has met his goal.

All goals can be measured, if you frame them the right way. Get creative if you need to and set a goal that you can measure in some way. Consider that all types of measurement are valid. That can be time put in, miles run, weight lost, or cigarette cravings resisted. Whatever it is, make sure to keep track of your measurements somewhere so you can refer back to them. Use your journal or your phone.

Tracking progress is essential to meeting a goal. It keeps you motivated and lets you know how much progress you are making each day. If you don't keep some record of your progress, it is much easier to abandon a goal or forget about it.

- Think about what type of measurement makes sense for your goal. It could be anything from miles run to books read, or even cats adopted.

    Measurement I will use:

    _____
    _____

The "A" stands for attainable. Make sure your goal is something attainable and within your control. If your goal is to buy a home, that's great. You can save money, talk to a real estate agent, and start looking at open houses. However, if your goal is to buy a specific house, you see that is not a good goal. It is not considered attainable, not because you could never get it, but because you cannot control if you achieve that goal or not. You may put together a great offer, but the seller may go with someone else's slightly better offer. You have no control, so you cannot call that goal attainable.

85

- Assess whether your goal is achievable. Think about what factors you have control over and which ones you don't. Make sure that your goal is more in your control than out of it.

Is my goal achievable?: _____

If your goal is not achievable, reframe it now.

New goal:

_____
_____

If your goal is achievable, then we need to decide if it is realistic. My weight loss goal is attainable; I am entirely in control of losing weight, barring any health problems. Since I am fortunate enough to be very healthy, I don't have to worry about that. However, I could still set an unrealistic goal.

Losing 100 pounds in 3 months is not realistic. It would require unhealthy and dangerous measures to even come close. Instead, losing 15 pounds in 3 months is a very realistic goal. I can achieve that while still staying healthy and not having to focus too much time or attention on it.

Make sure your goal is realistic. Unrealistic goals set you up for failure and can damage your self-esteem. Aiming high is good, but goals still need to be achievable. It is actively demotivating and counterproductive to set unachievable goals.

On the other hand, realistic and attainable goals build self-love by showing ourselves grace, and being fair to ourselves. These types of goals give us challenges that are just tough enough that we can feel good when we meet them, but not so tough that we are doomed to failure.

- Decide if your goal is realistic. Make sure it is something that will require you to push yourself slightly, but that it isn't so difficult that you are more likely to fail than succeed. Keep your goals moderately difficult.

Is my goal realistic?:_____

If your goal is not realistic, reframe it.

New goal:

_____
_____

The final requirement for a goal to be considered SMART is that it be time-bound. Time-bound simply means that the goal has an end date by which it should be achieved. This is helpful in two ways. First, it motivates you and gives you a time frame to strive for. Second, it helps to prevent never-ending goals.

Never-ending goals are demotivating because we can never achieve them, and they damage our self-esteem by denying us the confidence that truly achieving a goal gives. Goals are important, not just for their own sake, but because they help us to build confidence and self-love when we celebrate our achievements. Never-ending goals rob us of this chance to celebrate. So, make sure your SMART goal is also time-bound.

- Set a time limit for your goal. Do not let your time limit be so small that it makes your goal unrealistic. Also, don't set a timeframe that is so long that you may forget about your goal or lose motivation. The time limit on a goal should be short enough to light a fire in you, but not so short it causes stress.

My goal's timeframe:_____

Not sure where to start with your goals? CBT can help there, too. It is recommended that you first identify the goal and make sure it is a SMART goal. Don't worry too much about the time-bound part just yet, though.

Now, identify where you currently are. This is your starting point. It may be your current weight, the time it takes you to run a mile today, or how much you have saved for a big expense. That is your starting point. Don't be ashamed of it, or worry if you feel far off from your goal. Even if it takes time and a lot of steps, you can still get there.

- Recognize where you are now. Now that you know your goal, take a look at your starting point. Think about where you are, concerning your goal, and formulate, in a few sentences, a picture of where you stand now.

My starting point:_____

Now, start writing out the steps between your starting point and your goal. This doesn't have to be an exact plan, but it should be somewhat specific. It may be how many pounds you want to lose a week, how many runs you want to get in this month, or how much money you want to put away each pay period.

This step will help you formulate an idea of what kind of timeframe to put on your goal. Based on the steps you will need to take, you can more easily decide on the timeframe for your goal. You can also use them to start formulating a specific plan. Decide what days and times you will go out and run, figure out what expenses you will cut to save the extra money, or decide how many calories you need to eat a day to lose weight.

- Create your steps. The smaller and more detailed each step can be, the better. The idea is to come up with actionable, specific steps you can start taking immediately to reach your goal. If you want to get more specific or have more steps than there is room for here, then use your journal or record your plan digitally.

Step 1:

_____
_____
_____

Step 2:

_____
_____
_____

Step 3:

_____
_____
_____

Step 4:

_____
_____
_____

Step 5:

_____
_____
_____

Finally, write out your specific plan. Put it in your calendar, or make a note and keep it where you will see it daily. Use this as a reminder to follow your plan and stick to what you need to do to achieve your goal.

- Get started! Now that you have a goal, know where you're starting from, and have a plan to reach your goal—don't delay. Begin on your SMART goal as soon as possible. Continue to evaluate and record your progress, as you move toward your goal and take each step.

The first step I'll take:

_____
_____
_____

After the time has come, do some reflection. If you meet your goal, celebrate in a healthy way and show yourself some love. Write about what went well, what strategies helped you stick to your plan, and if you made any changes or adjustments along the way. Don't forget to also write about how you feel now that you've met your goal, and what it means to you to have achieved it.

If you didn't meet your goal, don't beat yourself up. Instead, take some time to reflect on how far you did come. Think about what you could have done better and how you might have been able to achieve it. Then, you can reset the goal and try again. This time, you will be starting with some progress and a better idea of what to do to be successful.

- Reflect on your goal and how the results turned out.

_____
_____
_____
_____

Takeaways

- CBT encourages us to set SMART goals.

- These types of goals support our self-esteem and help us make specific plans to reach them. SMART goals are more achievable than non-specific or never-ending goals.

- SMART stands for

    o   Specific

    o   Measurable

    o   Attainable

    o   Realistic

    o   Time-bound

- CBT also advises that once we make a SMART goal, we assess our starting point and come up with specific steps to move from our starting point to our goal in the timeframe we created.

This has been a big journey, and you've learned a lot. In the conclusion, we'll wrap everything up and talk about what you can do to continue working with CBT to improve your self-love. There will even be some exercises you can do to evaluate your progress so far.

Conclusion:

Going Further

Whatever good things we build end up building us. —Jim Rohn

Jim Rohn is definitely right, when it comes to CBT skills and new ways of looking at the world. You have built a lot of good knowledge and a firm foundation in CBT throughout this workbook. I am sure you have already seen success in decreasing social anxiety and toxic thinking. The techniques and new ways of thinking that you have learned can continue to be of use on your journey toward self-love and living your best possible life.

- Think about the successes you've had so far. Write about them here. This kind of positive reflection is important to keep up motivation, and to learn from what is going well.

My successes so far:

_____
_____
_____
_____

This book has taught you the basics of CBT, from the principle of the cognitive triangle to the dangers of automatic negative thoughts. You've learned about thinking distortions that cloud our judgment and increase anxiety.

This workbook has also outlined tools to build a better way of thinking. You've challenged and begun to change your negative core beliefs, worked on exposure therapy to lessen your anxiety, identified your values, and set SMART goals for moving forward.

Now that you are ready to move forward, I encourage you to continue using the CBT techniques you've learned. CBT is not about a once-and-done solution to anxiety or toxic thoughts. You have to keep applying the tools that CBT gives you, to make sure you maintain the gains you have made.

But, with continued work, you will make more and more gains in the areas of self-love and decreased anxiety. In addition to increased self-love and reduced anxiety, you will find that using your CBT skills gets easier too. Each time you practice a technique or catch a thinking distortion, it becomes that much more automatic.

Don't become discouraged if you have setbacks, or if it seems difficult to apply some skills and exercises. Changing your thoughts, behaviors, and feelings takes time. You developed social anxiety, or decreased your self-love, over a period of time. It will take time to undo that damage, and correct the core beliefs and distorted thinking you have developed.

- Write out a short plan of what you will do, if you become discouraged. You could look back at the progress you've recorded, talk to a trusted friend, reread parts of the workbook you found helpful, or (if necessary) contact a mental health professional.

If I get discouraged, I will:

_____
_____
_____

Remember that CBT has been proven, time and again, to work effectively for a variety of struggles. Keep working at it. Continue to repeat workbook exercises in your journal, talk to and work with trusted friends, catch your thinking distortions, and engage in new healthy behaviors. As your thinking and behavior change, your feelings will change, too.

If you find you are overwhelmed or are struggling too much, reach out to a therapist or mental health professional. It is not hard to find a therapist trained in CBT, because it is such a widespread and effective form of therapy. You can even use this workbook with your therapist, and ask for more guidance or resources on the topics I've written about.

The journey toward self-love and freedom from toxic thoughts can be a difficult one, at times. But, it is deeply rewarding. I can say for sure that CBT works to reduce social anxiety because it has worked for me, and I have seen it work for others in my research.

- Write out what will be the next step on your journey to self-love and freedom from social anxiety. It could be a book you want to read, a new goal behavior, a problem you want to solve, or an exercise you want to repeat.

My next step:

_____
_____
_____

Finally, decide on a way you will reward yourself for all the hard work you have put in while you worked through this book. It can be any type of healthy treat or indulgence. Maybe buy a new journal you love, give yourself a massage, or spend some extra time watching a favorite film. It is important to show yourself love by rewarding yourself for accomplishments. As adults, we don't often get pats on the back or praise for our hard work, so we must give it to ourselves when we earn it.

I will reward myself by:

_____
_____
_____

Use your new CBT skills. Set goals. Remember that changing your thoughts and behaviors will affect your feelings. Keep moving forward. I believe in CBT, because I know it works. I believe in the power of self-love, because it has transformed my life. And, I believe in you, too!

Book Takeaways

- CBT stands for cognitive behavioral therapy. It is a proven therapy for a wide range of issues, including social anxiety and low self-esteem.

- The cognitive triangle says that thoughts, feelings, and behaviors all influence each other.

- Because it is hard to control feelings with willpower, CBT focuses on cognition (thinking) and behavior changes to influence feelings.

- Automatic negative thoughts are the negative thoughts we have without trying to think of them. They can lead to thought chains that cause us to "spiral out." Questioning our automatic thoughts helps us make sure they are accurate and realistic.

- Thinking distortions are common ways that our thinking becomes clouded and unrealistic. CBT has identified over 30. Knowing thinking distortions can help us to correct our thoughts and make them more balanced.

- Core beliefs are the beliefs we hold to be true about ourselves, others, and the world. They, too, can be unrealistically negative and distorted. Correcting them to more realistic beliefs helps reduce anxiety and increase self-esteem.

- Exposure therapy is the process of slowly getting closer and closer to engaging in a goal activity that causes you anxiety.

- Discovering your values will help you live a life you love and feel good about. Knowing your values clearly also makes decision-making easier.

- The mind has an innate negativity bias. This bias can be countered by cognitive restructuring. Take a negative thought, think of its positive opposite, then combine the two into a balanced and realistic thought.

- CBT has a five-step problem-solving process. To solve problems the CBT way, you identify the problem, brainstorm solutions, list the pros and cons of the best solutions, use those to choose a solution and implement it, then reflect on how your solution worked or didn't work.

- CBT advises we use SMART goals when setting goals for ourselves. SMART goals are specific, measurable, achievable, realistic, and time-bound.

References

American Psychological Association. (2017a, July 31). *What is cognitive behavioral therapy?* https://www.apa.org/ptsd-guideline/patients-and-families/cognitive-behavioral

American Psychological Association. (2017b, July 31). *What is exposure therapy?* https://www.apa.org/ptsd-guideline/patients-and-families/exposure-therapy/

Arocho, J. (2015, November 23). *How CBT uses goal setting.* Manhattan Center for Cognitive Behavioral Therapy. https://www.manhattancbt.com/archives/544/cbt-uses-goal-setting/

Barrie, J. M. (1911). *Peter and Wendy : The story of Peter Pan.* Grosset & Dunlap.

Flannery, B. (2022, August 15). *Behavioral chain analysis: A CBT tool.* YouMeMindBody. https://youmemindbody.com/mental-health/Behavior-Chain-for-CBT-or-DBT-Why-You-Do-What-You-Do/

Jones, S. M. W. (2022, February 2). Solving problems the cognitive-behavioral way. *Psychology Today.* https://www.psychologytoday.com/us/blog/all-about-cognitive-and-behavior-therapy/202202/solving-problems-the-cognitive-behavioral-way

Keelan, P. (2013, May 13). *Cognitive restructuring: How to move from distorted thinking to balanced thinking to improve your mood.* Dr. Patrick Keelan. https://drpatrickkeelan.com/relationships/cognitive-restructuring-how-to-move-from-distorted-thinking-to-balanced-thinking-to-improve-your-mood/

Peale, N. V. (1952). *The power of positive thinking.* Prentice Hall..

Peale, N. V. (1959). *The amazing results of positive thinking.* Hind Pocket Books.

Schaffner, A. K. (2020, June 26). *Core beliefs: 12 worksheets to challenge negative beliefs.* Positive Psychology. https://positivepsychology.com/core-beliefs-worksheets/

Selva, J. (2018, April 23). *Values clarification in CBT and beyond: 18+ examples and tools.* Positive Psychology. https://positivepsychology.com/values-clarification/

Therapist Aid. (n.d.-a). *Cognitive Distortions* (Worksheet). Retrieved September 16, 2022, from https://www.therapistaid.com/therapy-worksheet/cognitive-distortions/

Therapist Aid. (n.d.-b). *The Cognitive Triangle* (Worksheet). Retrieved September 16, 2022, from https://www.therapistaid.com/therapy-worksheet/cbt-triangle/

Vaish, A., Grossmann, T., & Woodward, A. (2008). Not all emotions are created equal: The negativity bias in social-emotional development. *Psychological Bulletin, 134*(3), 383–403. https://doi.org/10.1037/0033-2909.134.3.383

Warhol, A. (1975).The philosophy of Andy Warhol: From A to B and back again. Harcourt Brace Jovanovich.

Image references

Bruna, B. (2018, January 5). *2018 here we come* [Image]. https://unsplash.com/photos/TzVN0xQhWaQ

Durant, Z. (2017, July 4). *Sunshine bath* [Image]. https://unsplash.com/photos/_6HzPU9Hyfg

Dziedzic, M. (2020, August 16). *Fire and Ice II: Crystal pyramid shot in studio with colored flashes* [Image]. https://unsplash.com/photos/nc11Hg2ja-s

Gios, J. (2021, February 6). *[White jigsaw puzzle pieces on brown marble table]* [Image]. https://unsplash.com/photos/SqjhKY9877M

Jodoin, M-O. (2017, April 14). *Hope* [Image]. https://unsplash.com/photos/TStNU7H4UEE

Pascual, R. (2018, November 28). *[Woman sitting near sea during daytime]* [Image]. https://unsplash.com/photos/SACRQSof7Qw

Simmer, J. (2020, February 26). *[Blue green and red plastic clothes pin]* [Image]. https://unsplash.com/photos/Vqg809B-SrE

Towfiqu Barbhuiya. (2021, October 2). *[Possible written on chalkboard]* [Image]. https://unsplash.com/photos/Jxi526YIQgA

Wang, J. (2015, June 4). *[Close up photo of gray stone pile]* [Image]. https://unsplash.com/photos/qG-hPxoAnRE

X). (2017, October 3). *[Woman climbing mountain]* [Image]. https://unsplash.com/photos/N4QTBfNQ8Nk

Printed in Great Britain
by Amazon